COLLINS GEM GUIDES

CATS

written by
Howard Loxton

D1513452

A NOTE ON NEW BREEDS

Despite the great variety of conformation, colour, pattern and fur among cat breeds new types are still being created, in the silver range especially there is opportunity for new development. Although it takes some time for breeds to become recognized some of those described here with provisional standards may have gained full status by the time you read this book. The final standards may vary slightly from those provisionally accepted.

Illustrations on pages 5-60 by Charles Garner

First published 1985

©Howard Loxton 1985

ISBN 0 00 458850 9

Colour reproduction by Adroit Photo Litho, Birmingham

Filmset by Wordsmiths, Street, Somerset

Printed and bound by Wm Collins Sons and Co Ltd, Glasgow

Reprint 10 9 8 7 6 5 4 3

Contents

Introduction

The domestic cat is a member of the genus *Felis* and very closely related to its other members which range from the Lion *Felis leo* and the Tiger *Felis tigris* to the Rusty Spotted Cat *Felis rubiginosa*, of India and Sri Lanka, which is only about 60cm (2ft) long from nose to tail tip, and the Flat-headed Cat *Felis planiceps* which lives on river banks in Borneo and southern Asia, and is even smaller, weighing only 2kg (4.5lb). At one time the big cats (the lions, tigers, leopards and jaguar) used to be given their own genus *Panthera*, because zoologists found a small variation in the development of a bone at the base of the tongue. In the big cats it forms a thread-like ligament, so that the tongue and larynx are quite loosely attached to the base of the skull. This enables the vocal apparatus to move freely, so that the big cats can roar, while the medium and small cats can only make comparatively feeble cries. On the other hand the little cats can purr continuously, whereas the big ones have to take a breath between each vibration.

Zoologists still place the long-legged cheetah in a separate genus, *Acinonyx jubatus* for although quite clearly another cat, and one which shares the arrangement of the vocal apparatus of the smaller cats, its difference lies in that after the first few weeks of kittenhood the cheetah can no longer retract its claws!

All the cats probably descend from a prehistoric feline now called *Dinictis*, which roamed the earth about 40 million years ago, and looked very like the modern cats. It had a smaller brain than they have but larger teeth: one of its immediate descendants was the sabre-toothed tiger which lived in the Pleistocene period, whose stabbing teeth were adapted to hunt the mammoth and the mastodon. Other descendants formed the branch which became the genus *Felis* with its 36 modern species.

From which of those species has the modern cat developed? It is possible that more than one kind of cat has been domesticated. In Egypt, where the first records of cats occur, mummified cats in ancient catacombs included some of the Jungle Cat *Felis chaus* but most of them are much more like *Felis lybica*, the African Wild Cat, and it is generally thought that this was the species that was domesticated, although the Jungle Cat does tame fairly easily and is sometimes kept as a pet in India and Nepal. The European form of the Wild Cat, sometimes classed as a separate species, *Felis sylvestris*, and sometimes as a northern race of the same species as the African cat, may also have played a part, if only by interbreeding with the already domesticated cats which are thought to have been taken to Europe from Egypt.

The European Wildcat does look very like a modern domestic tabby, except that it is bigger and has a rounded tip to its tail. The domestic cat, which is now usually classed as a separate species *Felis catus*, can breed with *F. sylvestris*, *F. lybica* and with some of the other smaller cats such as *F.geoffroyi*, Geoffroy's Cat, of South America, and the Rusty Spotted Cat.

There are other physical differences between the wild cat and the domesticated form, for instance, the domesticated cat actually has a smaller brain, but the main difference is that they are tame – and that the tameness appears inbred, although offspring of feral and wildcat crosses revert to the temperament of the wild cat and tend to adopt its solitary life.

However, the cat was only very recently domesticated in evolutionary terms, settling down with man long after the dog. The evidence is said to be in the cat's lack of pendant ears, which appear in many dogs and some farm animals. They were seldom encountered in cats until recently deliberately developed in the Scottish Fold (see page 102). It is probably only in the last hundred years that man has interfered in the

European Wild Cat

7

creation of the individual breeds and the cat is still very close to the wild animal. If early selection favoured rodent catchers this would reflect the cat's natural behaviour patterns. The status of the cat as still close to the wild is even reflected in British law for, whilst the dog owner is responsible for his or her pet's behaviour, the owner of a cat cannot be held responsible for anything it does because it is an uncontrolled wild animal. At the same time, although deliberate cruelty to any animal can be prosecuted, there is no requirement to take any action concerning a road accident involving a cat, whereas one involving a dog or a horse is reportable.

For many people the degree of independence and lack of domestication are part of the appeal of the cat, but cats have also developed a close relationship with humans and their interaction with us is an important feature of their appeal as pets, together with their intelligence and sheer physical beauty.

The Cat's Physique

Cat's are vertebrates – they have skeletons very like our own; they are mammals – they mate, females carry the developing young inside their bodies and give birth to live kittens, and they are carnivores – they eat meat, are hunters and their bodies have developed to meet the demands of an hunter's life.

The cat's skeleton has about 40 more bones than ours – most of them in the tail and spine, which makes their spine more pliant. More important differences are their much smaller collar bones, which enable the cat's forelimbs and shoulder blades to move much more freely, and the restriction of the movement of the rear limbs to a mainly vertical plane, enabling the muscle development to give them a very powerful spring. The cat can also turn its head

Cat skeleton

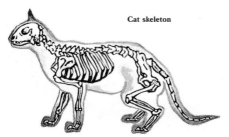

through nearly a full circle, its ears can move to focus on a sound and its eyes look in the same direction so it sees in depth. Its narrow chest makes it easier to balance on narrow ledges, because the legs are closer together, and the tail also aids its balance. The cat walks on its toes, giving an effectively longer stride and speeding movement, because only the small toe area has to touch the ground. The end joint of the cat's toes can be angled backwards to retract its claws which grow to sharp points, periodically shedding their outer layer to maintain their sharpness. It has a full coat of fur, often consisting of a downy undercoat with a longer topcoat.

A very effective muscular system operates the skeleton and the part of the brain that controls it is particularly well developed and linked with a highly responsive sensory and nervous system.

The cat can easily jump upwards to five times its own height but is less efficient jumping down. Usually it reaches down as far as possible before leaping, to shorten the distance and make the landing less heavy on its front paws. If a cat falls from a height it will twist its body to an orientation that results in a four-point landing, arching the back to cushion the landing. The flexible skeleton and lack of width enable it to squeeze through narrow places.

Cats can put on a considerable burst of speed but cannot run fast for long because they do not have the lung and heart power. As hunters they can never be certain where the next meal is coming from, so the cat must be able to gorge upon a kill one day and perhaps go hungry the next. For this reason the stomach and digestive system take up a large part of the space within a cat's body, reducing that available for heart and lungs. A resting cat will take about four times as many breaths as a human and will soon be winded when exerting itself. When hunting it relies more upon stealth and accuracy of attack than upon speed but it can freeze and hold a position in mid-movement to avoid detection.

Sight

The cat cannot see as much colour as we do, which makes it less easy for it to distinguish stationary objects, but a cat's eyes are efficient over a much wider range of illumination and they react to any movement. They cannot see in pitch dark – there must be some light to record an image – but the iris can open up to admit the maximum light, like a camera opened to a very wide aperture, and a reflective layer at the rear of the eye (found in most nocturnal animals) sends back any light not absorbed on its passage through the eye to register a second time. This enables cats to see when our eyes would register no light at all, whilst the narrowing of the iris to a tiny slit enables them to cope with very bright light. The cornea and lens are comparably larger and more curved than in the human eye, giving a greater angle of vision: a total field of 185°, although that is less than that of most prey animals which can see behind themselves without turning their heads. There is good overlap between the images seen by each eye so that cats can see in three dimensions and judge distance accurately, better than most other mammals·but not so well as humans. For some reason in Siamese cats and albinos the nerves do not feed all the messages from

Iris closed

Iris open

Nictitating membrane raised

12

the eyes to the correct part of the brain and they have less efficient binocular vision.

From the inner corner of the eye a translucent fold of skin, known as the nictitating membrane, can be raised to give additional protection against very bright light or dust. If it remains up it is usually a sign of illness, although it is said that eating a lot of grasshoppers also has the same effect!

Cats cannot focus well at very close distances (try bringing your hand against your face and see when you lose clear vision), so sometimes do not see what is literally under their noses, but register it through scent instead.

Smell and taste
Cats have a highly developed sense of smell. It does not seem to play as big a role as sight and hearing but is important in identifying things and communicating information, especially sexual information. It is scent that makes a newborn kitten struggle to its mother's nipples (its eyes will not open for about eight days). Although unfamiliar smells are disturbing to young kittens, as they grow up they seem to get a great deal of pleasure from scents that they like.

There are scent producing glands in several parts of their bodies, but especially by the anus, along the tail, around the lips and chin and on either side of the forehead. Cats mark their territory with secretions from these glands and unneutered males spray urine which also contains strong personal smells. When a cat rubs up against you affectionately it is at the same time marking you with its scent. You will often see a cat sniffing where another cat has been. It will be gaining information about the cat and will be able to identify the mark of cats it knows. Two cats meeting will sniff each other, reinforcing their recognition and feelings of security about each other and gathering other scent information – rather like having a chat about where they've been. A domestic cat will investigate you and your bags when you come home, smelling out all the scent messages (as well as what's in the shopping) and sometimes showing jealousy if you have made contact with other animals.

The nasal surface carrying cells sensitive to smell is twice the area of that in the human nose and in addition the cat, along with many other species including snakes and the horse but not man, has an additional scent organ opening into the mouth. Known as the Jacobson's organ, it registers both air-carried scents and those collected upon the tongue which can be transferred by pressing it against the opening. If you see a cat concentrating with a rather curious expression on its face, its mouth open and its upper lip curled back, it is almost certainly demonstrating what zoologists call the 'flehmen reaction', using its Jacobson's organ to concentrate on a smell it likes or finds interesting.

The senses of smell and taste are very closely related and the main taste buds of the cat are carried along the front, sides and back of the tongue. Cats are very sensitive to the taste of water. They do not usually like sweet things and it may be that the smell of food is more important to them than its taste. However, they tend to be very conscious of stale food and may refuse a bowl that has been left down too long.

The central surface of the tongue is covered with backward-hooked papillae – you can feel them rasping against your skin when a cat licks your hand. These scrape meat off bones, hold food and act as an efficient brush for removing dead fur from the coat. To drink, the cat may cup the end of its tongue into a ladle when drinking from deep liquid but it mainly relies upon the liquid adhering to the papillae.

The cat's teeth consist of tiny sharp incisors in the front, which can rip and scrape, flanked by large canines which can hold and kill prey and tear meat. The teeth further back can cut meat up into smaller pieces for the cat to swallow.

Hearing

The cat's hearing is both much more accurate and much wider in range than ours. It is an important way of locating small rodent prey by their squeaks and rustles of movement, and a cat can pinpoint with great accuracy the location of a sound. It does not hear low pitches quite so well as people and dogs do, but its upper register is higher than a dog's and at least an octave and a half higher than ours. Part of the inner ear is responsible for the sense of balance and it is thought that there may be something special about this since cats not only have very good balance but, unlike dogs and humans, never seem to get sea, car or air sick. It is also connected with their skill in making a good four-point landing when falling, though visual perception and touch sensors also appear to contribute and a deaf cat studied by one researcher proved to still have this ability. It makes a contribution to their reputation for 'nine lives', but does not make them invulnerable. From a height they may land with sufficient force to break a jaw or limb, and if they are dropped by a child without distance to manoeuvre, or slip off a ledge while half

16

asleep may not be able to right themselves – if a cat sleeps on a window ledge make sure there is a barrier to prevent it slipping off!

Touch

A cat's nose and paws (especially the pads) are particularly sensitive to touch and often used to investigate objects. The large area of the brain associated with the paws shows the measure of their importance, but all over the body there are touch receptors and the most sensitive of them are probably the vibrissae – the stiff hairs of the whiskers, eyebrows and at the back of the front paws – which react to the slightest change in pressure. They probably do not have to touch a surface but respond to air currents and changes in pressure caused by the presence of a surface. They help a cat to negotiate a space even when its eyes are inadequate.

Cat health

Cats can suffer from many of the same troubles and illnesses as humans – from fleas to leukemia – though they do not catch our form of influenza or the common cold. Sneezes, snuffles and a high temperature, have earned the common name of cat flu for two serious diseases, properly known as Feline Viral Rhinotracheitis (FVR) and Feline Picornavirus Infection (FPI), and are symptoms of both. They have to be treated with antibiotics and careful nursing. A vaccine is now available which will give some protection. Most serious of cat diseases is rabies (of which quarantine has kept Britain almost free) for which the symptoms include restlessness, dislike of light and sudden noises, and later vicious attacking behaviour. It is almost untreatable. Innoculation is available which may give some protection in countries where it is endemic and for cats being sent abroad from Britain. It is not permitted for British cats as part of the policy to keep the country rabies free.

However, the most frequent killer disease for cats is Feline Infectious Enteritis, or Panleukopenia, which is highly infectious. First symptoms are fever, vomiting, loss of appetite and loss of interest, the cat probably sitting hunched up in a corner. Effective vaccine gives protection and should be given to all cats, with booster shots at the proper intervals according to the form of vaccine used. Shows and boarding catteries will not accept cats which have not been vaccinated.

The most common health problems for cats are fleas, mild infestations of which can be treated with dusting powders and sprays, and internal parasites. Tapeworms, segments of which may lodge in the fur around the anus, looking like grains of rice, or appear in the faeces, or roundworms, which may be seen by very keen eyes as wriggling threads in vomit, are treated with pills. If you are uncertain collect a sample of vomit or faeces and put it in a plastic box or bottle and take it to the vet with the cat.

Diarrhoea or vomiting can be caused by the cat eating something that disagrees with it. Missing a meal may put that right but if it persists it should not be ignored. Any radical changes in behaviour, continued diarrhoea or vomiting, listlessness, excessive scratching or straining when excreting are indications that the cat may be sick and suggest a visit to the vet.

Do not ignore accidents and injuries. Cats' wounds usually heal rapidly but may sometimes heal over an infection, especially in the case of rodent bites and puncture wounds from a fight.

Caring for a sick cat you should follow your vet's instructions precisely. The cat will need a quiet, warm place to rest, away from noise, draughts and bright lights. Although it will want some attention you should not overfuss but let it rest. Make sure that you understand what medication or other treatment to give and, if you are not sure, ask to be shown how to give it.

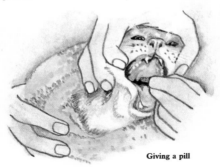

Giving a pill

To give a cat a pill, cup the head in one hand and squeeze gently with the fingers on either side of the mouth. It will open, allowing you to pop the pill far to the back. If you are afraid of the cat biting, pop it in on a spatula of wood or firm plastic (or you may be able to get a special dispenser from a pet store). Hold the jaw shut and stroke the throat until you are quite sure the pill has been swallowed. Watch the cat carefully when you release it in case it has been faking and spits the pill out later! Medicines are most easily given with a syringe or eye dropper. Pull down the skin at the side of the mouth and insert the syringe in the space between the front and back teeth then slowly release the liquid. Again hold the mouth shut and stroke the throat. Get someone else to hold an uncooperative cat and wrap it in a towel to stop it struggling.

Giving medicine

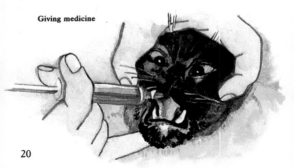

Understanding Your Cat

Cats are intelligent and fastidious animals, they like warmth, comfort and regular meals and can relatively easily be trained to fit into a home. Domestication of the cat appears to arrest some aspects of its development so that it does not become the solitary adult of the wild cat but shares its life with other cats or cat-surrogates (ourselves) and may stay very dependent upon its humans. This does not stop other instincts developing, for even a kitten will chase anything that moves.

The fights and games of kittenhood are practical training for adult life, though a built-in mechanism seems to stop kittens actually harming each other. Although all cats will stalk and pounce – whether after true prey, a leaf or a ball of crumpled paper – if they are taken from their mother before being taught the technique of the kill and the association between prey and food they may never associate hunting with catching their dinner.

Hunting

Cats will wait patiently beside a place where they expect prey to pass or to emerge, ready to pounce when the oppportunity occurs, or they will stalk carefully, taking advantage of all cover and keeping their bodies low to the ground and their ears down to

21

avoid a large silhouette. They may also move with bursts of speed, freezing every now and then to assess the situation and become invisible to their quarry. Cats will not usually chase after prey but will get as close as they can. They will quiver with tension as they wait for the exact moment to make a last dash, bringing them into range for a final spring, then, especially with larger prey, pouncing with the fore-paws and jaws while they keep their hind feet rock steady so that they can cope with any opposing action. They may immediately bite into the neck, or grasp the animal until they have located the exact place, but sometimes they will toy with a small victim, even letting it go and catching it again, behaviour which it has been suggested may be a form of practice for more difficult captures.

Small rodents are the cat's main prey and some become skilled at catching birds, although to do this the technique of the final spring has to be modified, or the bird will have taken flight. Cats can also become adept at catching fish, slipping a paw beneath and flipping them out of the water.

Grooming

Perhaps the most familiar action of any cat is washing, for cats seem to be continually grooming their own fur. They will often wash when not quite sure what to do, or if they want to pretend disinterest. For areas a cat cannot reach with its tongue it will moisten the back of a forepaw and use it as a sponge. Even shorthaired cats should be helped with grooming by regular brushing, and longhaired cats must be brushed and combed at least once a day to make sure that their fur does not develop matts and tangles. Firm stroking will also help to remove loose hairs and keep the coat in better condition.

The alignment of the hooked papillae on the tongue makes it inevitable that a cat will swallow some of the fur it removes and this can develop into furballs which it will regurgitate. Cats like to eat grass which can act as an emetic and help them bring these up. Cats' stomachs are not designed to digest grass but some cats seem to thoroughly enjoy eating it and it probably also makes useful roughage. For indoor cats

or those that live in an area with no gardens it is a good idea to grow some in a pot for them.

When you groom a cat you should also look out for any wounds or injuries, check that its coat is in good condition and free of parasites and that its ears and eyes are clean (wipe any dirt away with moistened cotton wool), that its teeth are in good order and its claws not overlong. Gums should be a healthy pink.

Don't let tartar built up on the teeth, if it becomes hard it will need chipping off by your vet. Overlong claws, which may develop if the cat does not exercise on hard surfaces, should be carefully trimmed with clippers (not scissors) taking great care to keep clear of the area where pink blood vessels show that the claw is still live. Never trim a cat's claws without being shown how to do it properly by a vet or an experienced owner.

Toilet and other training

Cats in the wild normally bury their droppings. It used to be thought that animals did this to hide their presence but it is possible that cats may do so to prolong their scent as a territory marker. Although burial makes the smell less strong it stops faeces drying out and so they keep their odour longer. An outdoor cat will often defecate outside its immediate territory but an indoor cat – and any cat whilst being established in a new home – must be given a toilet tray for it to use, with suitable absorbent 'soil' (commercial cat litter is widely available) which is frequently changed. A tray about 45cm (18in) long and 8cm (3in) deep is suitable. Models are available with covers to prevent litter being scattered outside.

Most mother cats teach their kittens to use a litter tray and a cat will usually just need to be shown it. To make sure lift the cat on to the litter and make a few scratching movements with its paws. If you see a

young kitten about to urinate or defecate pick it up and put it in the tray. It will soon learn to use it.

Chose a simple and easily recognizable name for your cat and, from the start, use it often when playing. To teach the cat to come when called associate 'come' with something nice by saying it whenever putting down food. Cats can be taught many things, including tricks, but they also learn by their own observation, though it can be frustrating if a cat refuses to see that if a door is just ajar it can hook a paw around the edge to make it open and instead pushes it shut in trying to grasp the doorknob in its paws!

Cats can be cunning and devious, and most will probably always enjoy a meal that they steal more than one they are given, but they can easily be taught the rules of the house – provided you do not keep changing them. No jumping up on to tables or surfaces such as cookers, no scratching of the furniture – whatever you want to teach – a stern word of disapproval may be enough to deter a cat. For stronger measures you can hit beside the cat with a rolled up newspaper. Never strike a cat beyond the blow of a wagging finger in admonition, you will create distrust rather than obedience. Praise and rewards are much more effective than punishment.

Since cats need to exercise their claws (they're not trying to sharpen them when they wreck your home) install a log or a scratching post or panel for them to use instead of your favourite armchair. This is especially necessary for a cat which is not allowed outdoors. Show it to the cat put its paws through a scratching motion against the surface and it will probably think it a welcome present.

Cat language

Although wild cats are usually solitary, domesticated cats, even feral ones, tend to live much more socially. Both toms and females have to find their place within an hierarchy. Toms gain theirs in fights – usually only an initial one to establish their rank, unless they are challenged for dominance or a newcomer has come into the area. Females gain prestige according to the number of litters they bear. Each cat has its own prime territory, although certain routes and areas will be shared and territory may even be occupied on a

Scratching post

time-share basis – mine in the morning, yours in the afternoon. At night cats allowed out will often congregate somewhere that is no one cat's specific territory and share mutual grooming sessions and friendly games, with no sexual encounters or hierarchical confrontation.

Cats communicate with a variety of soft chirruping sounds, which are particularly used to kittens and seem to indicate various forms of inquiry, affection and concern, sharper command sounds, cooing trills that toms use in courtship, a whole range of growls, snarls, spits and hisses when angry or giving warning, mating calls and the involuntary purr which seems to indicate contentment. The familiar meow and its variations are usually used to communicate with humans rather than with other cats.

People who are very close to particular cats will probably be able to interpret meaning from at least some of these sounds, and most owners will find demands for food or requests to be let out very easy to recognize, just as the cat itself will learn to respond to human sounds.

Even easier to understand, however, is the body language of the cat, presented through posture, facial expression and hair erection. When a cat is relaxed and happy it usually carries its tail high in the air, with the tip just slightly curled, especially in greeting. A position probably linked with kitten confidence when its mother used to clean its anal region. A twitching tail tip will usually indicate concentration and interest, but, if more of the tail twitches, it may be irritation, and a swish from side to side means it is getting really annoyed. The pricking of the ears is a clear indication of interest, and you may see an apparently sleeping cat manoeuvre its ears to catch a faint but interesting sound.

The whole body posture is full of information, especially in a confrontation between two cats or a cat and another species. A frightened cat will back away and try to be submissive, a confident one will advance and exert its dominance. In practice most present-ations are a mixture of the two, especially the familiar arched back angry stance – in which the rear legs are advancing and the front ones retreating!

Ears may be flattened to look smaller and more submissive, or pulled backwards to be less vulnerable to attack. Fur will stand on end to make a larger, more intimidating figure. Hair does stand on end when people are frightened and it is difficult to be sure whether this is a reaction of fear or aggression. Often

you will see a cat, and especially a kitten, rushing about with its tail bushed out like a Christmas tree - and even the short-furred orientals have enough to look a sizable bush!

Most cat confrontations usually consist only of such displays of intent with plenty of posturing, hissing and growling, without a real tooth-and-claw fight beginning. One cat eventually gives ground and the incident is over, though it may be a very long, drawn-out battle of wills before one of the cats will give up. If a serious fight does start and a cat finds itself really threatened it may risk rolling on to its back,

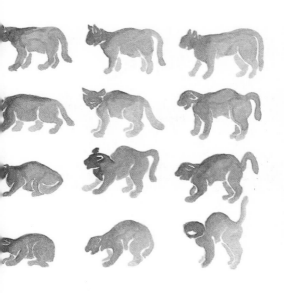

Aggressive and submissive responses are often taking place at the same time. In these poses the more aggressive attitudes are on the right. *Top row* Attention changes to suspicion. *Second row* Irritation turns to anger. *Third row* Warning changes to defiance. *Bottom row* Submission changes to hostility. Note the way in which front and rear of the cat are not necessarily indicating the same reaction.

exposing its vulnerable belly, partly a submissive posture from kittenhood but also one that enables it to lash out with its powerful back legs and dangerous claws.

Reproduction

Courtship and readiness to mate produces particularly recognizable behaviour. Subject to climate and the individual cat, females are on heat (ready to mate) for about four days if a tom is available, and about ten days if one is not, with an interval of two or three weeks between heats if they do not conceive. In practice some are receptive for only certain periods of the year. In Britain, for example, British Shorthairs tend to come in season early in the year for Spring births, and again six months later, while Siamese may come in season the year round. A few females manage to hide the signs of heat from their owners, perhaps because they know that kittens are not wanted, or at least that they will not be allowed out to meet a tom, but most begin to behave with more than usual affection. They roll around as though in ecstasy, rub against you and, if you stroke their backs, probably crouch and raise the tail, perhaps quivering when touched. All these are signs that a female is beginning to be interested in the idea of courtship. She will probably also make loud calls that sound more like someone in pain than a cry of love – and in the Siamese can be particularly unnerving, like a peacock's cry or a baby being murdered.

If you don't want a cat to have kittens then a female should be spayed. If you would like kittens (but not now) she must be kept closely indoors and away from potential mates when she comes on heat – and that means all windows, doors and other apertures tightly shut and double watchfulness when you go in and out to see that she does not slip past. If you want to breed a pedigree cat you will have to find an owner with a suitable tom, the breed club will be able to give addresses. If, however, you do not mind what the kittens are like then your female will have little difficulty in finding suitors. In fact they will probably already be lining up on your garden wall.

Females will not necessarily accept a male and may mate with a succession, producing kittens of more than one father in the same litter. After the exploratory overtures, when the female has decided to accept a tom, she will crouch and allow the male to straddle

Cats mating

her, taking the loose skin of her neck between his teeth, kneading her with his paws and moving backwards until they are in a position to copulate. The tom's penis, unlike that of other animals, is covered with short barbed spines which may be the reason for the sharp cry of the female on withdrawal. After mating the female will usually roll about on the ground, which is believed to aid fertilization. If you have arranged a pedigree mating make sure that no other males have access or you may end up with a mixed litter.

The gestation period for cats is approximately 64 days. A slight reddening of the nipples after about three weeks is the first outward sign of pregnancy. After a month it may be possible to feel the developing kittens – but it is wisest to leave that to your vet. The pregnant cat will demand more food as the embryos develop and her diet should include calcium and vitamin D.

A week or so before the kittens are due prepare a kittening box. A large cardboard box will do. Cut part of one side down to half and line it with newspapers. Put it somewhere quiet, warm and away from draughts. You will probably be able to tell when your cat begins to look for a likely nest. Place her in the box a few times and with luck she will adopt it. If she does not, note where she seems to have chosen and, unless a totally unsuitable place for kittening, move the box there: but remember this is not only where she will give birth but the spot from which she will raise her kittens. You will know that she has accepted the box when she begins to tear up the paper to make a nest and takes to sleeping there occasionally.

Signs of the imminence of birth are increased displays of affection, traces of milk on the nipples and a distended vulva, which may also produce lubricating fluids. The cat may also be seen to alternately scratch and squat. Now put a piece of clean old blanket in the box and cover it with a towel to keep it clean.

Some cats like their owners around to give them confidence (and even help) when the kittens are born, others prefer privacy. If you are there, try to check that after each kitten emerges the afterbirth follows. (It will usually be eaten by the mother.) If it is left within her body it can cause complications later. The cat will bite through the umbilical cord and wash away the membrane surrounding each kitten, which will then make its way to her nipples. Kittens may follow each other rapidly or have as much as an hour between.

It is always wise to take the mother to the vet for a check up before birth is due to make sure that there are no likely complications, and at the same time you can ask advice concerning any help you may need to give.

Kittens

Kittens use their sense of smell to find their mother's nipples and to locate the security of both mother and nest if they stray away. Hearing comes next and she

communicates with them in a whole range of squeaks and chirrups. Their eyes do not open until they are about eight days old, and it takes some time for them to actually come into use, although the kittens may be strugglingout of the nest long before that.

At first their life is eating and sleeping, and mother too, has little time for anything other than washing them, feeding them and resting in between. Most cats make good mothers and if a kitten is rejected it probably means that it is too weak to survive or that she cannot cope with such a large litter. If the litter is big you may be able to supplement her feeding with powdered milk specially constituted for cats - cow's milk is not really suitable, powdered baby milk is better if the proper mixture is not available. Bottle feeding small animals is a skill you need to be shown. Trying to raise a whole litter is a very demanding task and often fails if the feeder is not experienced. More successful raising of orphans results from finding a foster mother who can accept an extra kitten. It does not have to be a cat, sometimes a small bitch or a rabbit has raised a kitten and there are complementary cases of cats, for instance, rearing squirrel kittens.

It is sometimes easier to tell what sex the kittens are when they are very young, but do not handle them if it makes the mother unhappy. Viewed from the rear you can compare the placing of the anus and the sexual organs – it is always easier to compare kittens than to make a positive identification of one on its own. In females they will look closer together and be

Sexing kittens:
the female is on the left

the shape of a dotted (i). In males they look more like a colon (:).

Soon the kittens will be exploring everywhere. If mother thinks they are in danger she will call them back or even carry them back to the nest or some other place of safety, lifting them by the scruff of the neck held between her teeth. When you see them begin to show an interest in their mother's food, usually at about three weeks, you can offer them a little unsweetened evaporated milk mixed with about one third of the amount of boiling water. Then you can go on to creamed rice, strained baby foods and eventually scraped raw beef and steamed fish at five weeks, if the kittens are prepared to take it. By this time mother may be glad to be relieved of some of the effort of feeding them. Naturally she needs plenty of good food to help produce her milk and keep healthy herself.

Mother will teach her kittens a great many things, from using the litter tray to hunting techniques, but you can watch the kittens at play trying out all the skills which they need as adult cats. Provide them with safe toys – no sponge rubber which they might swallow, or sharp metal or pins, but crumpled paper, a table tennis ball, a cotton reel, things hanging on a string – or, better still, pulled along by someone at the other end. Chasing a leaf or ambushing another kitten, they will go through all the manoeuvres of hunting and fighting, pouncing as on a mouse or flipping a toy in the air as they might flip a fish out of water.

This is the time of learning, so do not spend all your time watching their games or joining in them. Take the chance to teach them some of the disciplines which you want them to have as adult cats while it still seems like play.

The History of the Cat

In ancient Egypt, perhaps long before their domestication, cats were venerated for their association with
various gods and goddesses, such as the sun god Ra
and the goddess Bast, in whose temple cats were
tended by priests and watched for any messages from
the goddesses that they might indicate by their
behaviour. Wall paintings show cats wearing collars
and with wildfowlers hunting from boats in the
marshes, seemingly trained as retrievers. Perhaps cats
were attracted to human settlements by rodents living
in the grain stores of the Egyptian civilizations, or by
the opportunities they offered for scavenging.
Whether they were encouraged as rodent catchers or
simply because of their role in religion, they were
treated with great affection and respect. Harming a
cat was a serious crime and a cat's death was mourned
by the owner's whole family. Hundreds of thousands
of mummified cats were sent for burial in a vast
underground cemetery close to Bast's temple at
Bubastis.

The export of cats from Egypt was not permitted
but they did reach Greece and Rome, and from Rome
were taken to the outlying parts of the Roman empire,
including Britain. The Roman agriculturalist Palla-
dius recommended that cats be kept to protect
gardens from mice and moles, and their value was
clearly recognized by the cultures that followed ⁻

Rome. Laws from Wales and Saxony both set high value upon the cat and it also found favour with Moslems, because Mohammed is said once to have cut off the sleeve of his garment rather than disturb a sleeping cat. For a time the cat was approved by the Christian Church as the only pet allowable for monks and nuns, its skin on death being used as a warm lining for nuns' clothing. But the connection of the cat with the old religions – for from its link with Bast it also became associated with Roman and other pagan deities – caused the later Church to link the cat with the Devil, and with witches.

Whilst peasants in rural France might believe in *matagots*, luck bringing cats who helped those who were kind to them (like the cat in the fairytale of Puss

Egyptian cat mummy and a bronze coffin for a kitten

Cats were linked with witches and the devil

in Boots), its nocturnal habits made others claim that it spent its nights on watch to warn gatherings of devils of the approach of intruders. At the suppression of their Order the Knights Templar were accused of worshipping the Devil in the form of a black cat and, as late as the 15th century, the Inquisition was instructed to root out cat worshippers and cats were persecuted.

It was not only in Europe and Egypt that the cat had religious significance. In Thailand and Burma it was believed that souls might enter into a cat between death and the next life. China had an agricultural god in cat form and in Japan cats were also linked with witches and there were stories of vampire cats. Devil cats in Japan could be recognized by having double tails. In both Japan and Europe there are stories of cats who could turn into women or women who could turn into cats.

When the hunt for witches spread from Europe to Britain and America in the 16th and 17th centuries any old lady living with her cat was likely to be charged with witchcraft – though Shakespeare designates it as 'harmless' and many references in poetry and literature show that the cat was a regular part of the domestic scene.

In Britain the black cat is now a symbol of good luck but in America and Europe it is the white cat that is lucky and black cats still have connotations of evil and bad luck, while in Japan the tortoiseshell cat, known as the Mi-Ke, is the lucky cat.

Japanese devil cats had forked tails

Fortunately the antagonism of the Church in Europe subsided, though cats still often had to suffer stupid cruelties and, even in the 19th century they were often regarded more as treacherous than lovable creatures. However, by the middle of the century a strong body of cat lovers was developing and a British cat fancier called Harrison Weir decided that it would be a good idea to hold cat shows, following the example of the already established dog shows, 'so that different breeds, colours, markings, etc, might be more carefully attended to, and the domestic cat sitting in front of the fire would then posssess a beauty and an attractiveness to its owner unobserved and unknown because uncultivated heretofore.'

In July 1871 the first major cat show was held at the Crystal Palace, London, organized and judged by Weir, who decided on the classes for competition and the 'standards of excellence' by which the cats would be judged. There had been earlier cat exhibitions – the first recorded is probably one in Winchester, England, in 1598 – but it was from the Crystal Palace show, and those that followed it, that there developed the modern Cat Fancy, as the world of organised cat enthusiasts is called. In America there had been exhibitions for Maine Coon cats in mid-century, but shows really became popular following one at Madison Square Gardens in 1895, and soon the idea was taken up in other countries. Various clubs were formed by the cat enthusiasts which sought to set standards for each type of cat and to establish rules for shows. In Britain, from 1910, they were united under one overall authority, the Governing Council of the Cat Fancy, until in 1983 a splinter group formed the Cat Association of Great Britain. In North America a number of rival organisations exist and the same is true of most other countries, though many are affiliated to the Fédération Internationale Féline.

British and North American shows are organised quite differently and the classes for competition and the ways of becoming a champion are not the same. In Britain the cats are judged at their pens, which are therefore kept plain with just a white blanket, a litter tray and a water bowl, with no identification beyond their number. In America cats are taken to the judge and their pens can be festooned with former trophies and decorative hangings.

Rules vary from show to show, and if you want to enter one you should study them carefully. You will want your cat to be in tip-top condition and need to groom it carefully. Cats must be immunised against the most serious cat diseases, to protect them and

other cats at the show, and naturally a cat known to be sick should not be shown. Shampoos, bran baths and talcum dusting can all help the appearance of the coat. There are books which will advise you on show preparation but finding another exhibitor to show you the tricks of the trade will be much more helpful.

The pedigree breeds

The earliest cat shows largely featured short-haired cats of different colours and longhairs were probably of the Angora type, though the more compact-bodied Persians later became more popular. With the aim of 'improving' colour and type (that is to say, making it conform with what the breeders thought desirable), more careful breeding began, pedigrees being carefully recorded and registered with the cat associations. Harrison Weir, from the start, drew up 'standards' for each type and all cat associations now have their agreed standards for appearance, coat, colour etc. They vary slightly from one organisation to another, but, in general, agree with the descriptions given in this book.

Some types of cat are naturally occurring, whether long established or the result of recent mutation, others have been deliberately created by cross-breeding. A wide variety of different types, patterns and colours now exist and new ones are still being developed. In general no form which has a tendency to physical defect is likely to be accepted, whether developed by selection for exaggerated characteristics or from mutant stock. For this reason a cat such as the Manx, which has been long established, would be unlikely to be accepted if presented for recognition today, and this is why the Peke-faced is not recognized in Britain.

The recognition procedure varies from organisation to organisation, some allow a provisional standard to be devised and kittens registered, but only exhibited in experimental classes until there is sufficient support for the new breed and evidence that it has no drawbacks. Fixed numbers of generations of breeding, of breeders or of individual animals may also be required. It can often take a long time for a new breed to be accepted.

Cat coats and colours

The basic cat fur is tabby, which is striped along each hair with bands of black and yellow. All others are modifications of this coat, either through the strength of the black pigmentation covering the yellow, its arrangement on the individual hairs, conversion into orange, or the suppression of colour to produce white or intermediate dilute shades. The tabby type hair (known as agouti) may result in either the blotched or striped pattern coats, spotting, or have the ticked effect of the Abyssinian cat, without an overlying pattern. Even when suppressed in the adult, tabby marking will often reveal itself in kittens.

Knowledge of cat genetics, the way in which such characteristics are inherited, has advanced considerably in recent years but new facts are still being discovered about it: for instance it is only recently that it was realized that silver fur is genetically different from a black-tipped white – and consequently silver fur cats can now be classed separately. Genetic inheritance depends upon the characteristics of dominant and recessive genes. Even though a cat may have a particular characteristic, because of a dominant gene, it can still pass on its recessive characteristics to its offspring, so that it makes an appearance later in the family tree, as with the matings shown below, using a black cat and a tabby. For this reason an exact knowledge of a cat's pedigree is necessary for planned breeding.

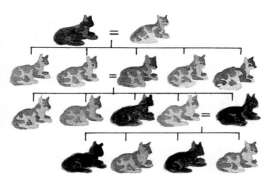

DOMINANT	RECESSIVE	OFFSPRING
Tabby	**Black**	**Tabby**
White	**Black**	**White**
Solid	**Pointed**	**Solid**
Black	**Blue**	**Black**
Shorthair	**Longhair**	**Shorthair**

49

The black coat colour can be diluted to become what is known as blue – a bluish grey – and two mutant forms have developed which provide a chocolate brown and a light chocolate. The orange colour – known as red in cat jargon – can be modified to cream. A combination of the dilute colours chocolate and blue produces a lilac or lavender coat. Some characteristics are always dominant over others as demonstrated in the chart on the preceding page.

Choosing a Cat

The main differences between cat breeds and varieties are those of appearance, details of which are given in the main part of this book. The kind of cat you chose will therefore be determined largely by aesthetic considerations – but there are differences in the attention which the main types need and, many owners and breeders claim, in their personalities.

There are three main types: shorthairs with the body type of the British and American shorthairs, shorthairs with 'foreign' body type (the 'oriental' cats) and longhaired cats. In all the temperament of the individual cats will be influenced by their parentage, conditioning and treatment so that an individual strain may show marked affection or intelligence and mistreatment or unfortunate experience may produce a nervous or neurotic cat. Early familiarisation with other cats, other animals and people will affect their tolerance of them, perhaps producing a personality that is counter to that expected for the type. The comments on personality that follow must therefore be treated only as generalisations.

Shorthairs British and European Shorthairs have a dense coat which protects them from cold and the American Shorthair has an even tougher coat. They do not need extensive grooming – a regular brushing to remove dirt and dead hairs and cleaning of the ears and eyes with dampened cotton swabs are all that a fit cat will need. They are intelligent, affectionate and rarely temperamental, with a quiet voice. Some breeds have less need for grooming than others.

Foreign, or **Oriental** cats, tend to be much more temperamental and demanding, especially the Siamese, which also has a very penetrating voice, unlike the Abyssinian which has a gentle voice even when on heat. Both Burmese and Siamese mature rather early and females may come on heat at six or seven months old. Orientals are especially inquisitve and like to be involved in anything that is going on: if they find it boring they will let you know.

Longhaired cats tend to be much more lazy and easy going, with gentle temperaments and quiet voices. They can adjust easily to a new environment provided that they feel secure, as though oblivious to what is going on around, provided they are comfortable. This gives them the ideal temperament for show cats. However, though they may not pester for attention, they do require daily grooming to keep their coats in good condition, for they can rarely deal with long hair without help, and tangles soon develop in their fine fur. Longhaired kittens have relatively short fur and the full length coat does not develop until the second annual moult. At that point the shedding of their longest fur leaves them looking quite shorthaired until the new coat gains length.

Maine Coon cats tend to have a more lively personality than the Persians and a coat that needs much less attention. The Nors Skaukatt is said to need only an occasional combing and also to be more people oriented. The long-haired versions of the oriental cats tend to keep the typical oriental personality, rather than gain that of the typical longhair.

Coat colour does not have any positive influence on a cat's character any more than it does on a person's, although blue-coated cats do have a reputation for gentleness, but in show cats black coats need care to avoid rustiness, often caused by too much sun, and white cats need attention to prevent the coat becoming stained.

Finding a cat

When they decide to have a cat, most people think of getting a kitten, but that should not be an automatic decision. There are many adult cats in need of a home and they have advantages in that you do not need to be around all the time to keep an eye on them and they are much less likely to get under your feet and trip you up. They will be already house trained and are less likely to scratch up your furnishings.

The main difference between pedigree cats and mongrels is that with a pedigree you can predict how a cat will look when it is adult and what its offspring will be like if it is bred. It will not be more intelligent or affectionate just because it has a pedigree and many people think that mongrels tend to be stronger and healthier. If you decide upon a pedigree you would probably do best to try to buy directly from a breeder or through a pet dealer who will act as an intermediary. Except for one or two breeders who do not want the bother of selling, or live in remote areas, most sell direct and their best kittens are not likely to be available waiting in a shop.

Selecting a kitten

If possible try to see kittens with their mother and litter mates. You will be able to assess the environment for cleanliness and freedom from infection and to see something of the mother's temperament. The interaction of the kittens will give you some idea of their personalities and health. Do they stand and run sturdily or are their signs of lameness? Are they bright-eyed with the nictitating membrane down, and free from any discharge? Are there dirty specks or a gummy substance in the ears which might indicate mites? Is there any sign of diarrhoea or of worms around the anus? Is there a pot-belly (another sign of worms)? Is the fur glossy and mat free? Check for the tell-tale black specks of flea droppings and for any sores on the skin. Is the inside of the mouth pink and healthy and is there a set of clean white teeth? If there

is any sign of sickness in a litter, especially if the breeder does not draw attention to it, it is advisable not to have any of them. Worms can be easily dealt with and it is usual to treat all kittens for them, so ask if this has already been done. If you have doubts insist that any purchase is conditional on a veterinary check-up, which is anyway a good idea for a new cat.

The liveliest and boldest kitten is not necessarily the best to choose, for the 'top cat' could be domineering and bossy and difficult to discipline. On the other hand, the runt of the litter, although it may attract your sympathy, is the most likely to have physical weaknesses. Often two kittens seem very attached to each other – if you are going to be out all day and there are no other household pets think of having two cats so that they can keep each other company when you are not there.

Unless you intend to breed it does not make a great deal of difference whether you have a male or a female, for you would be well advised to have them neutered – there are already many more kittens born

than there are homes for them. Neutering used to be carried out when kittens were only a couple of months old but now it is thought preferable to wait until they are approaching maturity. Ask your vet's advice and make arrangements for the operation to be carried out when she or he prefers. For males it is a simple operation that does not require major surgery, but for females more organs are removed and the cat will come back from the operation with a patch of fur shaved and a row of stitches which will have to be removed after a week or ten days.

Kittens should not leave their mother until they are weaned and at least eight weeks old, so, if you see them younger, you will have to reserve one and wait until it is old enough to collect. Make sure that you are then given the pedigree (if it is a pedigree cat) and its vaccination certificate (if it has already had its first set of jabs). You should also ask for a diet sheet so that you can continue with the same food and meals, gradually changing them as the kitten gets older. If you intend to breed or show your cat you will also need to register the cat and its change of ownership. The breeder will be happy to explain how to go about this.

Preparing for the new arrival

There are a number of things that you will need to prepare, ready for the collection of your new cat. First you need a carrying box or basket. These used to be traditionally made of wicker but now plastic-covered wire and fibreglass pet carriers are available which are more easily cleaned and disinfected. A carrier which opens from the top makes it easier to lift a cat in and out. If you have one that opens at the front you may find it easier to control the cat if you place the basket on its back and, with the opening upwards, lower the cat in, then right it. Zipped carriers are not a good idea, it is too easy to trap fur in the zip, and all carriers must be properly ventilated. Vets and pet shops often have cardboard carriers which are practical for shortterm use, though cats can scratch and chew their way out of them. A wire carrier or one of open wicker work should be lined with newspaper around the sides to keep out draughts if used outdoors. Never try to travel with a cat held in your arms. If they are frightened or inquisitive they may easily jump away and be lost or injured.

You will also need a litter tray and a box or basket lined with newspaper and a blanket as a cat bed – though you may find the cat would prefer to sleep on

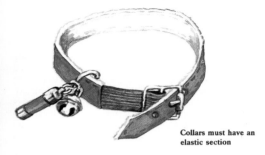

Collars must have an elastic section

yours. The cat should have an elasticated collar with a name tag in case it strays. The elastic will stretch, enabling the cat to free itself if it should get hooked up somewhere. The name tag can either be a disc or a cylinder in which a roll of paper with name and address can be placed. Some owners, afraid that their valuable cats might be stolen, have a number tattooed on the inside of the leg. A lead will give you control if you travel with the cat and you may even succeed in teaching it to go for walks with you.

Food and water bowls are also necessary. They should be shaped so that they do not tip over easily. Special ones are available which remain covered, to keep the food fresher and flyfree, until the cat steps on a panel in front which raises the cover. You also need a suitable brush and comb, nail clippers (if the cat is to spend most of the time indoors), and a scratching post.

Make sure that the great day for the kitten or cat's arrival is one when you can be there to give it attention, and when there will not be a great deal of noise and disturbance about the house. Although an inquisitive cat may enjoy exploring somewhere new, sudden removal from familiar surroundings, especially for a kitten leaving its mother and litter mates, can be very disturbing. Only introduce the cat to one room at first – and keep all doors and windows shut, just in case it panics and does a bolt. If there is an open fire make sure it is well guarded and if there is an empty grate stuff up the chimney with newspapers, cats have been known to climb up chimneys! Once it has settled in you can explore other parts its new home together, but do not let it out of doors for the first few days, unless on a lead.

For the first few nights a hot water bottle tucked under its bedding and a clock with a loud tick (such as a wind-up alarm clock) will act as substitute for the warmth of its mother and siblings and the tick will

Bowls should be non-spill

give the same sort of pulse as its mother's heart beat to provide a further sense of security. Remember to remove the water bottle before it goes cold, or instead get one of the small waterproof electric heating pads specially made for pet beds, and be careful not to wind the alarm part of the clock – you don't want it to give the kitten a fright by going off!

For cats in neighbourhoods where it is safe for them to be free ranging, a cat door will make it possible for them to come and go as they please. Most kinds have catches which will keep them shut if you need to keep the cat indoors, when on heat or after immunisation for instance. Some have catches which open only to the cat's own key – a magnet worn on the collar – and so, provided other cats in the neighbourhood do not have a magnet with the same polarity, will keep intruders out.

Cat door

Short-haired Cats

BRITISH SHORTHAIRS

The British Shorthair and the very similar European Shorthair are similar to the cats which you can see in many old paintings and are probably descended from the cats which the Romans originally introduced to Britain and western Europe, but the modern breed is a very specific type of cat. In the 19th century the general type was carefully bred to produce the sturdy looking British Shorthair of today which has a compact body of medium length set upon short legs – what is known as a 'cobby' look. It has a strong-boned skeleton which is well covered and powerfully muscled, but not fat. The chest is broad and the body deep from spine to belly. The short, strong legs have rounded paws and the forelegs should be straight. The back is carried level and the shortish tail is thick at the root, tapering only slightly to a rounded tip.

The head, set upon a short, thick neck, is shaped like an apple and has full cheeks. The nose is short, broad and straight, the chin firm and the ears small, with rounded tips and set well apart. The large, round eyes are fairly widely spaced. They are orange or copper in most varieties.

The fur is short and dense with a fine plush texture. It will rarely become badly tangled and is quite easy to groom. Hand grooming (heavy stroking) will remove quite a lot of old hairs, but regular brushing should not be neglected to remove dirt and dust and to keep the coat in good condition. A number of colour varieties are recognized.

Many non-pedigree cats appear to be very like the British Shorthair, but mongrels rarely have the correct combination of fur type, conformation and eye colour. Even pedigreed cats sometimes have faults such as a tinge of the wrong colour around the rim of the eye, too open a coat, too long a nose, face or legs, small eyes or pointed ears.

Tabby British Shorthairs The Wild Cat of northern Europe has a loosely striped coat and this form of 'tabby' marking is one of the most dominant among all cats. The name tabby is said to come from Attibiya, a district of Baghdad once famous for the making of tafetta or watered silk, a material which gives a very good idea of a second tabby pattern, now known as the classic or blotched tabby. This appears to have developed in Europe, where it was becoming common by the mid-18th century. A hundred years later it had reached India, and in long-established centres, such as London, predominates over the striped or mackerel type.

Like the blotched pattern, both spotted coats and agouti (or ticked) fur are thought to be mutations from the striped tabby. A narrow-striped 'lined' tabby also appears sometimes, which is thought to be a half-way stage between the mackerel and the agouti.

There are now strict regulations for the two recognized patterns, to one of which a tabby should conform. The classic has three stripes running down the spine, a butterfly-like shape across the shoulders, with spots within its wings, an oyster- or poached egg-shaped blotch surrounded by unbroken rings on the flanks, two necklace-like chains on the chest and evenly barred legs and tail. The face has pencil markings on the cheeks and an M-shape on the forehead. The mackerel tabby has the same markings on the head, legs and tail, but only a single stripe on the spine from which stripes run at right-angles down the sides.

Brown Tabby British Shorthair has a brilliant copper-brown coat with markings of dense black. The back

Brown Tabby British Shorthair

of the legs from paw to heel should be black too. Eyes may be orange, hazel or deep yellow, nose leather is brick red and paw pads either black or brown:

Silver Tabby British Shorthair (Mackerel pattern)

Silver Tabby British Shorthair (Standard, or Blotched pattern)

Blue Tabby British Shorthair

Red Tabby British Shorthair

Silver Tabby British Shorthair has silver fur with dense black markings, including black from toe to heel. Eyes are green or hazel, and paw pads and nose leather preferably brick-red, although black is permitted.

Red Tabby British Shorthair has deep red markings on a coat of lighter red. Lips and chin and the sides of the feet should be dark red. Eyes are copper, nose leather brick red and paw pads deep red.

Blue Tabby British Shorthair, so far only given a preliminary standard with the classic pattern, has deep blue markings on a bluish fawn ground. Nose leather and pads may be blue or pink. Eyes are copper, orange or deep yellow.

Brown Spotted British Shorthair

Silver Spotted British Shorthair

Spotted British Shorthairs Spotted cats are often seen among the indigenous cat populations of the eastern Mediterranean, but they are usually of the 'foreign' type, longer and slimmer than the British Shorthair. For the British show bench they must conform to the British type and have well-balanced, well-rounded spots which should be as distinct and numerous as possible. Triangular, star-shaped or rosette-shaped markings would not disqualify a cat, but the pattern must not look like the stripes of a mackerel pattern tabby broken into narrow or elongated markings. The legs should be spotted as well as the body, and the tail should be spotted or ringed. The face carries the same markings as the tabby: a

Red Spotted British Shorthair

Blue Spotted British Shorthair

letter M made by frown marks on the forehead, an unbroken line running backwards from the corner of the eye and lines of pencilling on the cheeks.

Spotted cats, then called Spotted Tabbies, with even their face markings broken into spots, were around at the end of the 19th century, but disappeared from the British show scene until the mid 1960s.

The coat of the Spotted British Shorthair is recognized in all the colours accepted for solid-colour cats, provided that they have appropriate spotting, but they are mainly seen in silver, brown and red, with markings, nose, paws and eyes following the colours given for tabbies.

Black British Shorthair This variety must have fur which is jet black to the roots without a single white hair in the coat. The eyes must be deep copper or orange, with no trace of green, and nose and paw pads should be black. Black kittens are often born with a rather brownish tinge, or even faint tabby markings, but they usually become solid black as they get older. Cats which bask in the sun a great deal will develop this rustiness and would be penalized for it in a show, although allowance will be made if they are still kittens. Black cats are considered lucky in Britain and are popular, but in some other European countries and in America their past association with the devil has linked them with ill omen.

Blue British Shorthair The British Blue, as it is usually known, often has the plushest of all shorthair coats and in fur and conformation most frequently approaches the ideal requirements for the British Shorthair type. Years ago, a dark slate blue fur used to be preferred, but now the standard specifies a medium to light blue or an even shade all over. The eyes should be a rich copper or orange and nose leather and paw pads should match the coat colour.

This variety has a reputation for being very gentle and placid and usually extremely intelligent.

Chartreux This French breed used to be more massive than the British Blue but it Britain is now considered identical with no separate standard. Some

**Blue British Shorthair
(British Blue)**

Black British Shorthair

69

American associations make it a separate variety requiring a less round head with larger and higher set ears. In France the eyes may be green and the fur any shade of blue.

White British Shorthair White Shorthairs must have a pure white coat with no creamy tones or trace of any other coloured fur. Their nose leather and paw pads

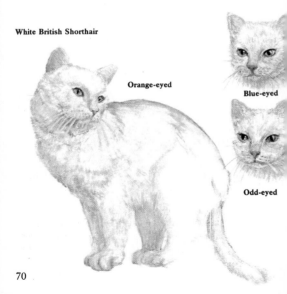

White British Shorthair

Orange-eyed

Blue-eyed

Odd-eyed

are pink but these cats are genetically white, not albino, and there must be no pink to the eyes, which may be blue, orange or one eye of each colour (known as odd-eyed). Blue eyes with white fur is genetically accompanied by deafness, but since all kittens are born with blue eyes, which change to their adult colour later, it is impossible to determine this at birth without testing their hearing. Kittens (especially those with other colours in their recent ancestry) may have traces of another colour, often appearing as a dark smudge on the top of the head, which is permissible in kittens even at shows, and this will almost certainly guarantee that their hearing will be unimpaired. White cats also have a greater tendency to polydactylism – having extra toes.

White is a dominant colour, so why are there not more white cats about? They are rare in feral populations, perhaps because, in addition to the deafness factor, they are more noticeable to their prey when hunting and to hawks and others who may prey on them when kittens. White patching, however, is very persistent in all cats.

In America, and other countries where black cats were of ill omen, it was the white which was thought to bring good luck.

Red British Shorthair For many years the solid red was dropped from the British Shorthairs because it was so difficult to produce a cat without tabby markings. However, a preliminary standard has now been re-established requiring a cat that has as few

Cream British Shorthair

Red British Shorthair

tabby markings as possible and no sign of white anywhere. Eyes are copper or orange and the nose leather and paw pads are brick red.

Cream British Shorthair The ideal Cream Shorthair has an even-coloured coat of pale cream, lighter shades being preferred, but this is difficult to achieve. Often there is a fawn or orangey look or traces of tabby markings persist, although kittens with markings may lose them when adult, unless a spell of very hot or very cold weather makes them temporarily reappear. Hazel-coloured eyes were once permitted, but for a long time the standard has insisted on a rich copper or orange colour. The nose leather and paw pads should be pink.

Chocolate British Shorthair Another variety with only preliminary status, the Chocolate may be any shade of rich dark brown. It must not look like the Havana (page 126) but be of full British Shorthair type. Eyes are copper, orange or yellow and nose leather and paw pads the same colour as the coat or pinkish. Kittens may have tabby markings which should disappear when they develop their adult coat.

Lilac British Shorthair The preliminary standard for this variety requires a coat of frosty grey with a distinct pinkish tone, so that the overall appearance is lilac. Eyes are copper, orange or deep gold and the nose leather and paw pads pinkish.

Lilac British Shorthair

Chocolate British Shorthair

73

Bi-colour British Shorthairs These cats have a white coat patched with a second colour which may be either black, blue, red or cream. The patches should be evenly distributed and form not more than two-thirds of the coat, with not more than one half white. The patching must extend over the face, where a white blaze running from the cat's forehead down over its nose is a desirable feature. A pattern which is

Red Bi-colour British Shorthair

Black Bi-colour
British Shorthair

symmetrically balanced is preferred and there should be no stray coloured hairs in the white area or ticking or barring on the coloured areas. The eyes should be brilliant copper or orange and the nose leather and paw pads should be pink against white fur, or follow the colour for solid-colour cats of the patching colour.

Cream Bi-colour British Shorthair

Blue Bi-colour British Shorthair

75

Tortoiseshell British Shorthair The Tortoiseshell coat is black brilliantly patched with red and cream in all parts of the body, face, legs and tail, with a good balance maintained between all three colours. Tortoiseshell patterning is very varied but, though the colours should be clearly defined over the whole cat, the standard now requires that there should not be any obvious patches of a particular colour. The three colours should merge into each other, with the exception of a short, narrow blaze on the face, which is permitted if not encouraged. Nose leather and paw pads may be either pink or black or a mixture of both. The eyes should be brilliant copper or orange.

The breeding of tortoiseshells is complicated by the fact that they are nearly always female – and males, when they are born, are almost all infertile – although there is a record, dating from the beginning of this century, of a pair of tortoiseshell toms both fathering kittens. Because of the sex-linking of the colour tortoiseshell females have to be mated to a male with different British Shorthair pattern: a solid colour black, red or cream. Tabbies cannot be used because they would pass on their pattern, and reds with a heavy trace of tabby must equally be avoided. Since the mother will also carry solid-colour genes the litter will almost certainly include solid reds and blacks as well as tortoiseshell kittens.

Sometimes tortoiseshells are born with very dark coats, but their colours usually become brighter as they grow older and it is these kittens which often show the finest markings when they become adult.

Although the use of tabby males is avoided the red and cream in the tortoiseshell pattern are thought to genetically reflect the light ground colour and darker markings of the red tabby, but the exact distribution of colour develops at the embryo stage and is not genetically predetermined.

Tortoiseshell kittens may also appear among the offspring of a mating between an all-black cat and an all-red cat, for the red cat is already carrying the tabby pattern in its genes.

Tortoiseshell British Shorthair

**Chocolate Tortoiseshell
British Shorthair**

**Lilac Cream
British Shorthair**

Chocolate Tortoiseshell British Shorthair This is a variety that has been given a preliminary standard that requires a coat with a balanced mixture of chocolate and rich red over the whole cat. The eyes are copper to gold and the nose leather and paw pads are chocolate or pink. or a mixture of both.

Lilac Cream British Shorthair A cat with a coat of mingled lilac and cream has also been given a preliminary standard. It should have copper to gold eyes. Nose leather and paw pads should be lilac or pink, or a mingling of both.

Blue Cream Shorthair In this variety the two colours, blue and cream, softly intermingle in the coat. They must not form sharply defined patches, nor should there be a blaze upon the face, nor any areas of single unbroken colour, or of tabby markings or white fur. The cream and white should be evenly balanced over the whole coat. The eyes are copper or orange. The nose leather is blue but the paw pads may be either blue or pink or a mixture of both colours.

The coat of the British Blue Cream is exactly contrary to that required of the same coloured American Shorthair, which has to be clearly patched.

Tortoiseshell and White British Shorthair This cat's coat pattern combines the red, cream and black patching of the tortoiseshell with a partly white coat. The three-colour tortoiseshell should cover the top of the head, the ears, cheeks, back, tail and part of the

Blue Cream British Shorthair

Colourpoint British Shorthair

flanks, with the patching clearly defined and a white blaze on the face desirable. Nose leather and paw pads may be pink or black, or a mixture of both. There should be colour patching on the paws but the underparts of the body, the chest, legs and chin should be white. The eyes are copper or orange.

Like the Tortoiseshell, this is a variety that is almost always female. Males of other varieties must be used for breeding: blacks, reds and black and red bi-colours are the most suitable.

Blue Tortoiseshell and White British Shorthair The preliminary standard for this recent variety asks for blue, cream and white evenly balanced in the coat, with the top of the head, ears, cheeks, back, tail and part of the flanks all patched. Eyes are copper to deep gold, nose leather and paw pads blue and/or pink.

Colourpointed British Shorthair This is a cat for which the preliminary standard requires the full British type, but with a clearly defined mask and points on the face, legs, ears and tail like that of a Siamese. Body colour is light cream or ivory, depending upon the colour of the points, following the standards of the Siamese (pages 112-23), which may be seal, blue, lilac, red, cream, blue-cream, chocolate tortie, lilac cream or tabby versions of these colours. Eyes are always blue.

Blue Tortoiseshell and White British Shorthair

Tortoiseshell and White British Shorthair

Smoke British Shorthair Smoke cats have a pale silvery undercoat, mainly hidden by a topcoat of a darker colour. When they move the undercoat shines through. Black and blue topcoats were the first to be recognized in the British Shorthair, but now any of the colours of solid-colour varieties is acceptable. With all, the eyes should be bright orange or yellow and the nose leather and paw pads should match the colour of the topcoat.

In this coat, while one gene supresses colour and creates the white undercoat, another increases the tippping of the topcoat to a full colour. However, this can vary, so some smokes are almost indistinguishable from solid colour cats and in the shorthair the undercoat is much less noticeable than in the longhair smokes.

Black Smoke British Shorthair

British Tipped Shorthair

British Tipped Shorthair In this variety both the undercoat and the topcoat are white, but the topcoat hairs on the back, flanks, head, ears and tail are all tipped with colour to give a sparkling effect to the fur. The legs may also be slightly tipped, but the chin, stomach, chest and undertail should be as white as possible. Once known as the Shorthair Chinchilla, but recognized as the British Tipped Shorthair in 1978, the tipping may be any of the colours recognized for solid coloured British Shorthair cats, including brown, chocolate and lilac. The nose leather and paw pads should either match the colour of the tipping or be pink. Eyes should be orange or copper in colour, except for black-tipped cats which have green eyes.

83

AMERICAN SHORTHAIRS

The first pedigree short-haired cat to be registered in the United States was an imported British Shorthair, recorded by the CFA at the beginning of this century, but since then a distinctly different type of cat has developed in America, influenced by the hardy non-pedigree shorthairs and even the Maine Coon, which was a favourite of 19th century American cat fanciers. Known for many years as the Domestic Shorthair, since 1966 it has been given the name of American Shorthair. A medium to large cat, it has a muscular body with a somewhat longer look than the British cat and longer legs, giving it a less square and cobby shape. The head is less round than the British Shorthair, closer to a heart shape, and set on a neck of medium length. The round-tipped ears are larger and more widely set, but less open at the base, and the large eyes are wide-open, but with a hint of a slant at the outer edge. The cheeks are full, the muzzle square and the chin firm. The tail is medium long with a thick base and tapers to a blunt tip.

The fur is short and thick, harsher than that of the British cat – a soft or fluffy coat would be a show fault – and a wide range of colours are recognized, though not all the cat organisations in North America recognise the full range of colours that have been bred and shown. Usually tough and hardy cats, they have a reputation as affectionate and intelligent pets.

The CFA standard describes the general effect of the American Shorthair as of a trained athlete 'lithe enough to stalk its prey but powerful enough to make the kill easily' with legs 'long enough to cope with any terrain and heavy and muscular enough for high leaps.'

White American Shorthair The pure glistening white coat of this cat is matched with bright blue or orange eyes – or with one of each – and, as in other white cats, blue eyes may also be genetically linked with deafness. The paw pads and nose leather should both be pink.

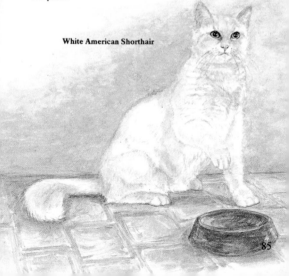

White American Shorthair

Cream American Shorthair

Black American Shorthair

Black American Shorthair The Black American Shorthair must have coal black fur with every hair a dense black from root to tip and with no hint of a rusty tinge or a smoke undercoat. Nose leather must be black, although the paw pads may be black or brown. The eyes should be brilliant gold in colour.

Blue American Shorthair A light shade of blue is preferred in this variety of the American Shorthair and it must be sound to the roots, with a level range of tone from nose to tail tip. An even and sound darker hue is more acceptable than a patchy or unsound lighter coat. Nose leather and paw pads should be blue and eyes a brilliant gold.

Blue American Shorthair

Red American Shorthair

Red American Shorthair It is difficult to breed red-self cats with no trace of tabby markings (which is why, until recently, they were not recognized in the British Shorthair) and they are nearly always present to some degree in this cat, although ideally the coat should be an even colour throughout. Nose leather and paw pads should be brick red and the eyes a brilliant gold.

Cream American Shorthair An even coat of buff cream, the colour going right to the roots and with no shading or markings, is the ideal for this cat, with lighter shades preferred. Nose leather and paw pads are pink and the eyes a brilliant gold.

Tabby American Shorthairs The American Shorthair is recognized in a wider range of colours than the
British cat, but all may be either the standard
(blotched) or mackerel (tiger) pattern with the markings following the specifications given for the British
tabbies (page 62).

Silver Tabby American Shorthair is probably the most
popular, and certainly one of the most attractive of all
the tabbies, with a ground colour, including lips and
chin, of clear silver and dense black markings. Paw
pads are black, nose leather brick red and eyes either
green or hazel.

Brown Tabby American Shorthair has a coppery brown
ground colour with markings in dense black. The lips
and chin should be the same colour as the fur around
the eyes and the back of the legs black from paw to
heel. Paw pads may be black or brown; the nose
leather should be brick red and the eyes brilliant gold.

Red Tabby American Shorthair has deep red markings
on a lighter red ground with brick red nose leather
and paw pads. Eyes are brilliant gold.

Blue Tabby American Shorthair has a pale bluish ivory
ground colour marked with a deep contrasting blue
and an overall warm fawn tone. Nose leather and paw
pads are rose and the eyes brilliant gold.

Brown Tabby American Shorthair

Blue Tabby
American Shorthair

Silver Tabby
American Shorthair

Red Tabby American Shorthair

89

Cream Tabby American Shorthair has a pale cream ground colour. Its markings must be sufficiently darker to give a good contrast but the whole coat should still remain within the dilute colour range. The nose leather and paw pads are pink and the eyes brilliant gold.

Cameo Tabby American Shorthair has colour-tipped fur producing red markings over an off-white ground colour. The nose leather and paw pads are pink and the eyes brilliant gold.

Parti-color American Shorthairs Also known as Bi-colors, these cats have a white coat which is

Cameo Tabby American Shorthair

Cream Tabby American Shorthair

Parti-color American Shorthair

Van Pattern American Shorthair

patched with a second colour which may be black, blue, red or cream. The patches are clearly defined and with no brindling. The nose leather and paw pads are the colour appropriate to the patching of the cat, or pink, and the eyes should always be golden yellow.

Van Pattern American Shorthair This is another type of bi-coloured cat, named after the similarity of its patching to that of the Turkish Van (see page 174) in its restriction of colour to the head, tail and legs, with only one or two small patches on the body. In other respects it is the same as the usual bi-coloured cats.

Blue Cream American Shorthair

Blue Cream American Shorthair Unlike the softly mingled colours of the British Blue-Cream, the American standards require a blue coat with solid patches of cream, clearly defined and appearing on both the body and the extremities. Nose leather and paw pads may be pink or blue, or a mixture of both. Eyes should be bright gold. The Blue-Cream is actually a pale version of the tortoiseshell pattern (facing page) in which dilution genes make the black into blue and red into cream.

Tortoiseshell American Shorthair The tortoiseshell is a black coated cat which is liberally and evenly patched with cream and red. The patches should be well-defined and without brindling, appearing on body, legs and face, where a blaze of red or cream is desirable. Nose leather and paw pads can be pink or black, the eyes should be brilliant gold. Since this variety is almost always female, the few males usually being infertile, breeding requires outcrossing to solid colour cats (see page 76).

A chestnut tortie, with the black replaced by brown is also recognized by some associations.

Tortie Tabby American Shorthair, also known as the Patched Tabby or Torbie, has a coat pattern not

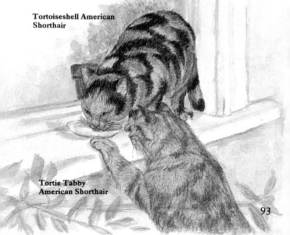

Tortoiseshell American
Shorthair

Tortie Tabby
American Shorthair

93

Tortoiseshell and White American Shorthair

Calico American Shorthair

recognized in Europe. Tabby pattern replaces the solid black areas and may sometimes be brown instead of black.

Tortoiseshell and White American Shorthair In some cat associations this cat's coat is like that for the British Tortoiseshell and White – being tortoiseshell on white. Bib, belly and paws must be white. White on the face is optional, but at least one third of the body should be white. Eyes are gold and nose leather and paw pads pink or black. The standards of associations differ, in some this variety is replaced by the Calico, in others both forms are recognized.

Calico American Shorthair Some of the American associations give this name to a cat like the British Tortoiseshell in coat pattern but others require a cat that has a white coat patched with red and cream in which, although there is a predominance of white on the underparts, there is not a distinctly white or distinctly coloured patched part; some standards describe it as looking as though it has been dropped in a pail of milk. Calico can also be used to describe a cat patched with only red and black and lacking cream. Eyes should be gold in all forms.

Dilute Calico American Shorthair is like the Calico, except that its colour patching is made up of blue and cream instead of red and black.

Dilute Calico American Shorthair

Chinchilla American Shorthair has a pure white undercoat and the lightest of black tipping, giving a sparkling silvery look to the back, flanks, head and tail. The chin, stomach and chest must be pure white, though the legs may be slightly shaded. The skin around the eyes outlines them in black, the paw pads are black and the lips and nose are also outlined in black, but the nose is brick red. The eyes are rich emerald or blue green.

Shaded Silver American Shorthair is a slightly darker version of the Chinchilla, with dark tipping on the spine, shading to lighter tipping and then to white underparts. The legs are the same tone as the face.

Shell Cameo American Shorthair Cameo colours are the red equivalent of the Chinchilla and the other black-tipped coats and this, the lightest version, is sometimes known as the Red Chinchilla.

Shaded Cameo American Shorthair or **Red Shaded** has slightly darker tipping than the Shell Cameo, graded from dark on the ridge of the back to white on the chin, chest and stomach. The legs should be the same tone as the face. Eye rims, nose leather and paw pads are rose; the eyes are brilliant gold.

Smoke American Shorthair has a topcoat so heavily tipped that the undercoat shows only when the cat moves. The narrow band of white at the base of the fur on mask, legs and tail can be seen only if it is parted. It may be blue, red or black (*overleaf*):

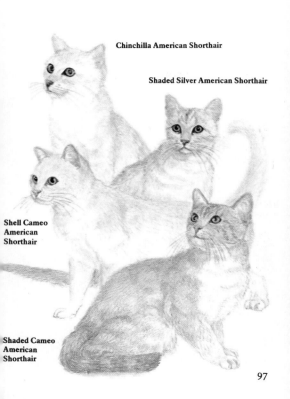

Chinchilla American Shorthair

Shaded Silver American Shorthair

Shell Cameo American Shorthair

Shaded Cameo American Shorthair

97

Black Smoke American Shorthair has jet black tipping, black pads and nose leather and brilliant gold eyes.

Blue Smoke American Shorthair has blue tipping, nose leather and paw pads and brilliant gold eyes.

Cameo Smoke American Shorthair, or *Red Smoke*, is heavily tipped with red. The eye rims, nose leather and paw pads are rose and the eyes brilliant gold.

Blue Smoke American Shorthair

Red Smoke American Shorthair

Black Smoke American Shorthair

MANX

The Manx is a cat without a tail. One story claims that it was lost when shut in the door of the Ark of Noah, others tell of the cat being brought by ancient traders from Japan or swimming ashore from a wrecked ship of the Spanish Armada – what is not disputable is that it has been established for a very long time on the Isle of Man, in the middle of the Irish Sea between Britain and Ireland. The taillessness is due to a dominant mutation which prevents the tail developing.

However, taillessness is not the Manx's only feature. They also have longer back legs than front, so that the hindquarters are carried higher than the back, though this is often countered by the bending of the rear legs. The rump should be very rounded, like an orange. The head should be like that of the British Shorthair in the British cat, with a straight nose, but in America some breeders prefer a definite dip in the nose. The ears are larger than the British Shorthair's and set higher on the head.

The Manx coat consists of a thick undercoat and a longer outercoat. Its texture is soft and open, rather like that of a rabbit – and the longer back legs give it a rather rabbit-like gait too! They may be any of the colours acceptable for a British Shorthair with appropriate eye colour.

The mutant gene which causes the taillessness can also produce other problems for the cat. It can affect other vertebrae in the spinal column and a malfunction of the sphincter sometimes occurs. In fact, if an embryo carries the mutant gene from both parents it will die in the womb, and even when only one mutant gene is carried there is still a larger than average number of still births and early deaths among kittens, mainly because of malformations such as fused vertebrae, and spina bifida is not uncommon.

Since cats with two manx genes do not survive there are quite a number of kittens born in Manx litters which have tails or vestiges of tails. While the true Manx should have a hollow at the end of the spine, kittens are often born with tails of varying length. In Britain both Stumpy (short-tailed) and Tailed Manx are now recognized varieties within the

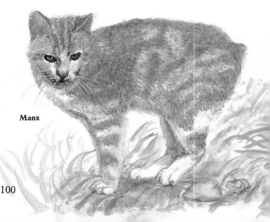

Manx

breed and in America some organizations recognize as many as five different types: Rumpy (tailless), Riser (with a small number of vertebrae which can be felt or seen), Stubby (with a distinct and moveable short tail) Longy and Tailed. Sometimes a Rumpy cat will have a tuft of fur like a vestige of a tail and this is acceptable provided that it does not contain cartilage or bone.

Although most cats use their tails as an aid to balance, the lack of one does not seem to affect the Manx to any great extent. Its long back legs give it a powerful spring and help it to cover ground more rapidly when running.

Tailed Manx

Rumpy Manx

Stumpy Manx

SCOTTISH FOLD

Most wild animals have pricked (upright) ears and only in species long-domesticated do they droop, like those of a spaniel dog. There are mentions of drop-eared cats in some old natural histories and in 1796 the *Universal Magazine of Knowledge and Pleasure* claimed that in China 'which is an empire very anciently policed ... domestic cats may be seen with hanging ears.' Talk of a drop-eared domestic breed in China persisted, although only one certain record of a drop-eared Chinese cat is known. An isolated drop-ear appeared in 1938 and the next record was not until 1961, when a kitten in Scotland was found with drop ears. The new breed was established from this mutant Scottish cat.

In Britain the Governing Council of the Cat Fancy refuses to register Folds – it was originally thought that they might have hearing defects and trouble with ear mites, neither of which seems to be true, although it is wise for owners to check that their cats' ears are kept clean. More seriously, some of the breed showed a thickening and shortening of the tail (which some breeders found apppealing) but this might also be accompanied by a thickening of the limbs and a crippling overgrowth of cartilege at the joints. Opposition to the type continued in Britain, although a kitten whose ears had not begun to droop (they are pricked at birth, the droop beginning to show at about four weeks) won a prize in a British show in 1971. Scottish Folds exported to the United States attracted attention and a following, although some breeders shared the British concern regarding limb deformities, and in 1976 the Cat Fanciers Association accepted them for registration, provided that any hybridization was only with American Shorthairs. Full championship status was given in 1978. The CFA standard requires ears 'set in a cap-like fashion to expose a rounded cranium' giving a preference for small, tightly folded ears. The Scottish Fold may be any of the colours and patterns recognized for the American Shorthair.

Scottish Fold

BOMBAY

This American variety is the result of crossing Black American Shorthairs with Burmese (of the American type, see page 154). The head is more rounded than the Shorthair, showing its Burmese blood, which also gives the cat its silky sleek fur, but its colour is black to the roots, with a look of shiny patent leather. The round eyes are set fairly wide and are yellow to deep copper, with the deeper colour preferred. There is a well-developed muzzle and a definite break on the nose. Nose leather and paw pads are black.

Bombays are said to have an even temperament, though retaining some of the foreign type's playfulness and liking for human company.

Bombay

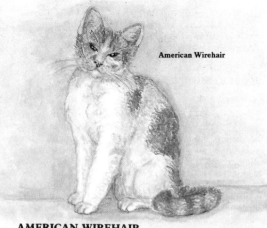

American Wirehair

AMERICAN WIREHAIR

Descended from a mutant farm kitten born in Vernon, N.Y., in 1966, this breed has its longer hairs (guard hairs) hooked at the tip and crimped along the shaft. This makes the coat dense, springy and resilient, and also coarse and wiry to the touch. It has been described as rather like sheep's wool. The medium to large body is well-rounded with a level back and the medium legs end in compact oval paws. The round head has prominent cheekbones and a slight whisker break, with the nose profile forming a gentle concave curve. The eyes are round with a slight upward tilt. Long-coated individuals have ringlets of fur. Colours are the same as those recognized for the American Shorthair.

EXOTIC SHORTHAIR

This breed came about when American breeders began to introduce Persian (Longhair) blood into their America Shorthair lines. This began to create too different a type of American Shorthair and, after the American Shorthair standard was laid down in 1966, it was decided to create the Exotic Shorthair as a separate breed. It is basically a short-haired Persian, although the coat is not so short as in the other shorthaired breeds. It is closer to the British Shorthair in appearance than to other American cats and, before the British Shorthair was given recognition as a breed in North America, some organisations registered it as an Exotic.

This is a chunky, cobby cat, its body set on short strong legs with large, round paws which have close-set toes. It looks massive both on shoulders and rump and has a round face set on a short thick neck. Its nose is broad and shorter than that of the British Shorthair and although, in the early days of the breed, the standard once specified a straight nose, it should now have a definite break. The cheeks are full and the chin well-developed. The round-tipped ears are small and set low on the head and far apart, tilting slightly forward. The tail is usually carried without a curve and at an angle lower than the back.

The coat is of medium length, dense glossy and soft textured, retaining the fullness of the Persian whilst reduced in length. It should be even with no feathery hair on the ears or tail and no tufts between the toes. It is accepted in a wide range of colours: black, white (in blue, orange and odd-eyed varieties), blue, red, cream, chinchilla, shaded silver, shell cameo, shaded cameo, black smoke, blue smoke and cameo smoke, bi-colours, both mackerel and standard tabby (in brown, red, silver, cameo and cream), tortoiseshell, blue-cream, calico and dilute calico.

Exotic Shorthair

SPHYNX

The Sphynx is an 'hairless' cat developed from a mutation which appeared in Canada in 1966, though other hairless cats have been known elsewhere. In fact, when adult, it does have a covering of soft downy hair, perceptible only on the large ears, muzzle, tail feet and the male's testicles. Although not of oriental stock they have a foreign-type body with a long tapering tail, neat oval feet and a rather wedge-shaped head. Their skin should be taut and wrinkle free except for the head. A rather barrel-shaped chest gives them a bow-legged look. They may be in any of the colours accepted for short-haired cats. They like a warm environment.

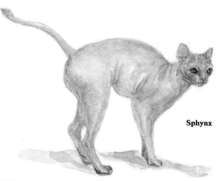

Sphynx

REX

The make up of a Rex cat's coat is quite different from the fur of other cats which consist of: (1) *Guard hairs*: long thick hairs which taper evenly, which both protect the coat and are the ones raised when a cat's fur 'stands on end' (2) *Awn hairs*: curving hairs with thickened, bristle-like tips, which grow in groups, and (3) *Down hairs*: fine crinkled hairs, which also grow in groups. In most cats there are many times more down hairs than guard hairs, but the fur of the Cornish Rex consists almost entirely of crinkly down hairs and awn hairs modified to look like down hairs, and all shorter than usual, while the Devon Rex has all three types, but so modified that the effect is much as for the Cornish.

The first record of a cat with Rex fur dates from 1946, when a cat was seen among a feral group at a German hospital in East Berlin. It produced kittens in the 1950s and eventually some of the German stock were taken to America. They contributed to the development of the American Rexes, but isolated Rex mutations also occurred in Ohio in 1953 and Oregon in 1959. Meanwhile, in Britain, a Cornish farm cat produced a rex-furred kitten in 1950, and ten years later a similar one was born in the neighbouring county of Devon – although in fact they actually have different genetic make-up and cannot breed together.

Cornish Rexes, exported to America before the native mutations were discovered and compatible with the German, formed the basis of the American

Cornish Rex

breed. The CFA did not recognize the existence of both Devon and Cornish until 1979, but some associations acknowledged both earlier.

In Britain the coat of Rex cats can be any colour with appropriate leather and eyes, which may also be Chartreuse, green or yellow, except for Siamese patterned Rex (Si-Rex) which must have blue eyes. In America Rex cats are not officially recognized in lavender, chocolate or Siamese points – although Si-Rex, are widely bred in America, as in Europe. Rex should have crinkly whiskers and eyebrows but these are sometimes short or even missing.

Cornish Rex These cats are derived from ordinary shorthaired cats – the first Cornish Rex was a single kitten in a litter born to a Tortoiseshell and White at Bodmin, father unknown, and about half of its own kittens had curly coats. The Rex has a longer, body than the British or American Shorthairs, much more like the Siamese. It also has the foreign type's long straight legs, small oval paws and long tapering tail. It has a slightly wedge-shaped head with large high-set ears, which have rounded tips, and oval eyes.

Devon Rex Mating Cornish or German cats with Devon produces only plain-coated kittens, although from the second generation some Rex coats appear. To be sure which strain a cat carries when planning a mating breeders have selected for cats with the features of the original Devon mutant: a head shape unique among cats, large oval eyes, a short nose with a definite stop, full cheeks, prominent whisker pads and huge ears.

Devon Rex

Foreign Shorthairs

SIAMESE

The Siamese are probably the best known of the cats of 'foreign' type and very typical with their long lithe bodies and wedge-shaped heads, but even more obvious to most people is the way in which the extremities of their bodies have dark colour in contrast to their pale bodies.

The Siamese are one breed with a name that really does link with their history for, even if it was not their country of origin, cats of this type have been known in Thailand for centuries. In the National Library at Bangkok is a set of manuscripts – *The Cat Book Poems* – that were saved from the sack of the old Thai capital of Ayudha by Burmese invaders in 1676. It includes pictures of a number of different types of cats, dogs and birds. One type of cat, the *Vichien Mas*, is like an extreme form of the modern Siamese: it has dark colour only on the ears, paws and tail andjust a little colour around the nose and whisker pads.

Siamese seem to have had a special place in the Thai court and a Bhuddist belief, that on the death of a very spiritually advanced person their soul would leave the body and enter that of a cat, and only on the death of the cat would it enter paradise, seems to have been the reason for the carrying of a cat during the coronation of a Thai king as recently as 1927. The cat represented the soul of the preceding king.

The first European record of a 'pointed' cat does not occur until the end of the 18th century 'when a German explorer and naturalist, Peter Pallas, published a picture of a Siamese-like cat with a chestnut brown body and dark points which he had seen in the region of the Caspian Sea in 1794.

When actual cats with Siamese points reached Europe is not sure. A pair of Sealpoints presented to the British Consul General in Bangkok in 1884 were taken to London and exhibited in 1885 – but this was not the first appearance of cats like this, for they were seen at a show in 1871 (the first show of a modern type). Unlike the drawings in the *Cat Book Poems*, but like that published by Pallas, they were much rounder in the face than the modern Siamese (though Pallas describes a cat with a longer nose than the European type.

Modern Siamese

The modern British standard demands a medium-sized cat with a long, svelte body, with the legs proportionately slim and the hind legs slightly higher than the front ones. The feet should be small and oval

113

and the tail long and tapering and free from any kind of kink. The head is long and well proportioned, with plenty of width between the eyes, and it narrows to a fine muzzle, offering a straight profile with a strong chin and a level bite. The large ears are pricked and wide at the base. The eyes, which are always blue, slant downwards towards the nose. In America an extreme foreign type is preferred, in Europe the cat is not usually quite so extreme.

The Siamese coat pattern consists of a pale coat with dark markings (known as points) on the tail, lower legs, and ears, and spreading across the face outwards from the nose are lines of colour linking the dark face 'mask' to the bottom of the ears. The colour should not run down over the throat or form a hood over the cat's head. Patches of colour on the belly, white patches on the feet or white 'spectacles' around the eyes would all be considered faults on the show bench. The fur is fine and sleek and lies very close to the body. In winter it often grows a little longer but, except in kittens, it should never be fluffy, although many breeders favour a soft, rather than a harsh texture.

Kittens are born with no colour markings apparent and have very fluffy fur. The first sign of their adult pigmentation appears as a smudge around the nose, becoming gradually more defined as a cat gets older. With age, many Siamese actually become very dark on the body, especially upon the back, but the difference between mask and paler coat can still be clearly distinguished.

Seal Point Siamese

Siamese often have a very harsh voice and can be very demanding of their humans. They usually mature very early compared with other breeds. They used to be considered rather delicate cats but, if they come of healthy stock, they are as hardy as most of their fellow breeds.

Seal Point Siamese was the first of the Siamese colours to be known in the west and this is the colour illustrated in the *Cat Book Poems*. It is genetically a black cat which the factor which restricts the colour to the face and extremities also dilutes it slightly to become a deep and lustrous brown, like that of the darkest Black skin tones. The body colour is cream shading into a pale warm fawn on the back. The paw pads and nose leather should be the same colour as the points. The eyes are a deep clear blue.

The earliest Siamese standard referred to the kink which so often distinguished the tail of the breed and which was the reason for a number of legends – that it resulted from being twisted around a goblet while guarding it, or from keeping a princess's rings on its tail. Today such kinks, or the crossed eyes which used also to appear in the breed, are considered faults.

Blue Point Siamese, the second colour to be recognized in America in 1932 and in Britain four years later. The body colour is glacial white, shading into blue on the back with the same cold tone as the

Blue Point Siamese

points but lighter in shade. Nose leather and paw pads should be blue.

Chocolate Point Siamese were not recognized in Britain until 1955 (1951 in America), but had certainly appeared much earlier, often being rejected as poor quality Seals before they found favour for their own colour. This is like milk chocolate on the points, with a body colour of ivory and any shading the colour of the points. Nose leather and paw pads should be blue.

Lilac Point Siamese, or **Frost Points** as they are still called by some associations in the United States, are produced when Chocolate Point Siamese are mated with Blue Points. They gained official recognition in America in the mid 1950s and in Britain in 1960. The body colour is off-white – the British standard describes it as magnolia, and allows some shading to

al Point Siamese

Chocolate Point Siamese

tone with the points. American standards ask for a milk or glacial white, verging on white, with no shading at all permitted. The nose leather should be a pinkish grey and the paw pads faded lilac or, in the ACAF, cold pink.

Red Point Siamese have a white body which, if there is any shading, may have a slight apricot tinge on the

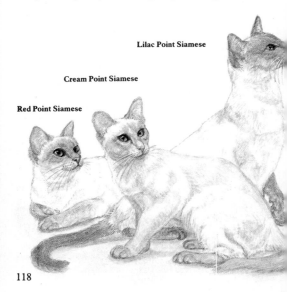

Lilac Point Siamese

Cream Point Siamese

Red Point Siamese

back. The tail, ears and mask should be a bright reddish gold and the legs and feet may be the same reddish gold or apricot. Red-pointed Siamese (then described as Orange Points) were shown in Britain in the early 1930s, but the variety known today was developed after World War II by both American and British breeders (using a red tabby in the United States and a tortoiseshell cross in Britain). In Britain official recognition had to wait until 1966 – a previous suggestion of recognition as Foreign Shorthairs having been rejected by the breeders – and in America they have never been accepted as full Siamese but Siamese but since 1964 they have been registered as Colorpoint Shorthairs (see page 125).

Cream Point Siamese, developed even more recently and also not recognized as a Siamese variety in America, is a further dilution of the Red Point. It should have a white body colour, any shading on the body being only the palest cream, with points that are the colour of clotted cream, growing warmer on the nose, ears and tail but only towards an apricot tinge and never becoming a hot shade. Nose leather and paw pads are pink. Since it is almost impossible to produce a cat devoid of markings, barring and striping in the mask and points is not a serious fault. Tabby-marked cats are identical in appearance to Cream Tabby Points.

Tortie Point Siamese, generally treated as Colorpoints in America, may have tortoiseshell markings made up of either seal, blue, chocolate or lilac as the main colour, mingled with red and/or cream on the points, including the ears. Their body colour and that of the nose leather and paw pads should be the same as those of cats with solid points of their main colour. The distribution of colour within the points is random and immaterial but should not include ticking or barring of any kind.

All the tortoiseshell forms are only found in female cats so they must be bred with cats of other colours and this delayed the development of the variety until later than that of the Red and Tabby Point Siamese. (For illustrations of other colour variations see pages 123-5.)

Tortie Point Siamese

Tabby Point Siamese, known in America as the **Lynx Point**, gained recognition in Britain as a Siamese variety in 1966, but most American associations place it with the Colorpoints. Because some people felt 'tabby' a rather ordinary name for such an aristocratic cat it was sometimes known as Lynx in Britain too. It is recognized in the whole range of colours accepted for Siamese cats: Seal, Chocolate, Blue, Lilac, Red and Cream. The tabby markings may also be mottled with the Siamese equivalents of the tortoiseshell colours – seal and dark cream, lilac and cream and blue and cream – to produce the tortie-tabby points.

All the Tabby Point colours have a pale body coat, preferably free from markings, even on the neck and back of the head, although there will usually be some

Tabby Point Siamese

121

body shading, especially with Seal Tabby Points, and older cats in particular will often show barring or spotting on the body in the same way that solid-pointed Siamese go darker. The tabby markings appear in all the points: the legs carry clear stripes, the tail is ringed and the mask has pencil lines on the cheeks, running outwards from the eyes, and an M mark on the forehead. The ears are solid colour except for a faintly lighter patch which looks as though someone has left a thumb print on the back of them. Nose leather and paw pads should conform to the standards for the equivalent solid point colour, or be pink. (The Red Tabby Point is illustrated with the Colorpoints, page 124.)

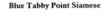

Blue Tabby Point Siamese

Tortie Tabby Point Siamese

Seal Tabby Point Siamese

Cream Tabby Point Siamese

Lilac Tabby Point Siamese

123

Red Lynx Colorpoint

Lilac Cream Colorpoint

124

COLORPOINT SHORTHAIRS

This is the name used by some North American cat associations for cats which are treated as full Siamese in Britain: Red Point, Cream Point, Tabby or Lynx Point and Tortie Point in all their colour forms – Seal Lynx, Chocolate Lynx, Blue Lynx, Lilac Lynx, Red Lynx, Blue Cream, Seal Tortie, Chocolate Tortie and Lilac Cream Point.

They are all of extreme foreign type with lithe slim bodies, long legs, long noses in wedge-shaped faces, long tapering tails and short close-lying fur.

Colours not illustrated here are shown under their names as Siamese (pages 118-123). Although identical to the Siamese in all respects except colour and pattern, they are considered by the bodies that class them as Colorpoints to be too different to be grouped with the classic Siamese.

Chocolate Cream Colorpoint

HAVANA (HAVANA BROWN)

First recognized in 1959 as the Chestnut Foreign Shorthair, this is the solid colour version of the Chocolate Point Siamese, but with green eyes. The American cat, recognized as the Havana Brown, was not crossed back to the Siamese, as was the British type, and has a rounder muzzle, a distinct stop level with the eyes and round-tipped ears. The eyes are chartreuse and the nose leather of a rosy tone.

**Havana Brown
American type**

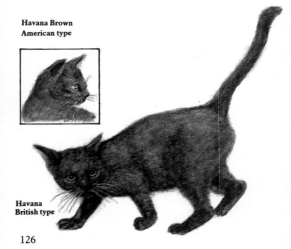

**Havana
British type**

FOREIGN TYPE (Self-colour)

Solid colour cats of Siamese type are called Foreign in Britain, whilst those with spotted, tabby and ticked coats are known as Oriental Shorthairs. The Havana, described opposite, is one of the same group in its British form.

Foreign Lilac (Lavender Oriental Shorthair) Cats

with a lilac coat appear only when both parents carry genes for blue and genes for chocolate. Individuals with this frost-grey coat with its pinkish tone appeared during the creation of the Havana cat. The British cat is of perfect Siamese type, and like the other oriental shorthairs is a solid colour Siamese in which the colour inhibition does not operate. It has pink paw pads and green eyes. Most American associations place this colour with the Oriental Shorthairs and the ACA standard asks for a slightly heavier cat than the Siamese.

Foreign Lilac

127

Foreign White (White Oriental Shorthair) This is a Siamese type cat in which the factors which restrict colour to the points have been so strong that all colour has been suppressed. They were created by breeding Siamese with short-haired whites. The British Foreign White must have blue eyes but in America the White Oriental Shorthair may have blue or green eyes and even orange eyes are not heavily penalised in shows. Since they do not carry a double dose of the dominant white gene, but have the colour inhibiting gene of the Siamese, they do not suffer from deafness as do many blue-eyed white cats. They are not albino, although an Albino Siamese is also known – in Britain it is usually known as a Recessive White and has not been recognized, in America both it and the Foreign White are placed with the Oriental Shorthairs.

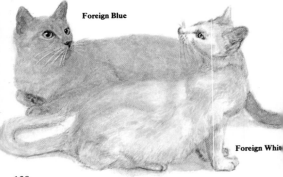

Foreign Blue

Foreign White

128

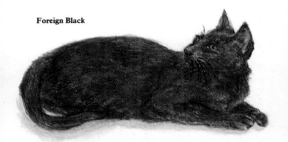

Foreign Black

Foreign Black (Ebony Oriental Shorthair) This is a Siamese type cat with a solid coat of lustrous black fur. In Britain it is a separate variety known as the Foreign Black but in America it is grouped with the Oriental Shorthairs. The eyes are green – though the Ebony, in America, is allowed to have amber eyes. Here the inhibiting factor is totally removed from the black so that not only is the restriction of colour to the points ended, but the dilution which produces seal has also gone, resulting in this solid, shining black coat.

Foreign Blue In Britain this is another svelte, solid coloured cat of the Siamese type. The Blue should have green eyes and solid blue nose leather and paw pads, though a pinkish blue is permissible in kittens.

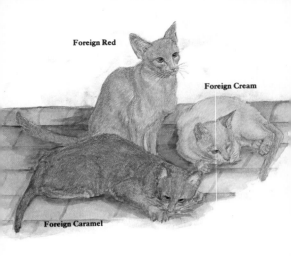

Foreign Red

Foreign Cream

Foreign Caramel

Foreign Red A preliminary British standard has been issued which requires a warm toned red coat for this cat with pink nose leather, paw pads and eye rims. The eyes may be all shades from copper to green, but green is preferred.

Foreign Cream A preliminary British standard asks for cool cream fur coupled with pink nose leather, paw pads and eye rims. The eye colour ranges from copper to green but green is preferred.

Foreign Cinnamon A preliminary British standard describes this cat's coat as a warm cinnamon brown. The paw pads may be solid brown or pink, but the nose leather and eye rims must be cinnamon. The eyes must be green.

Foreign Caramel Cool-toned bluish fawn to the roots is the way the preliminary standard describes the coat of this cat, which, like all this group of solid coloured cats, shares the basic Siamese physical type. Its nose leather, paw pads and eye rims are light tan brown and the eyes must be green.

Foreign Cinnamon

ORIENTAL SHORTHAIRS

In North America Oriental Shorthair is the name used for the solid coloured cats of Siamese type which in Britain are known as Foreign White, Foreign Black, Foreign Blue, Foreign Red and Foreign Lilac, but the breed also includes many other colour varieties which are not recognized in Britain. The coats of Oriental Shorthairs may also be Blue, Chestnut, Red, Cream, Silver, Cameo, Ebony Smoke, Blue Smoke, Chestnut Smoke, Lavender Smoke or Cameo Smoke, together with Tabbies of both classic and mackerel pattern in Ebony, Blue, Chestnut, Lavender, Red, Cream, Silver and Cameo, while Tortoiseshell type coats can be Blue-Cream, Chestnut-Tortie and Lavender-Cream as well as the standard red, black and cream tricolour. Other colours are being developed, including paler shades of brown such as the Cinnamon and Caramel seen in Britain.

All these cats have green or amber eyes, except the White Oriental Shorthair, which alone should have green or blue eyes (and must not be odd-eyed). Oriental Shorthairs have the conformation, coat texture and character of the Siamese and are in all respects other than their overall colour or/and pattern, similar to their pointed relations, although some people claim that they tend to have a softer voice.

Silver Oriental Shorthair

Cameo Oriental Shorthair

Tortoiseshell
Oriental Shorthair

Silver Tabby Oriental Shorthair

133

EGYPTIAN MAU

Mau is the ancient Egyptian name for cat and the spotted coat of this breed recalls that of some of the cats depicted in ancient papyrus and tomb paintings – cats which it is claimed were probably its ancestors. Spotted cats are not uncommon in the eastern Mediterranean but they are not necessarily of the type of these Egyptian Mau. The breed was developed by American breeders but was not their creation; it had its origin in cats from Cairo. A silver female taken to Rome was mated with a male already there. The female, with

Pewter Egyptian Mau

Smoke Egyptian Mau

a kitten from that and another from a further mating, were entered in a cat show in Rome before being taken to the United States in 1956. Twelve years later Mau gained full championship status in America.

This unique cat has an oriental look combined with a rather cobby build. The head has a more gentle contour than the Siamese, the wedge shape being slightly rounded. The eyes are almond shaped and slope slightly upwards at the outer corners, but fully oriental eyes are considered a fault.

The coat is long enough to allow each hair to carry two or more bands of ticking. The first cats introduced were Silver and Bronze but several colours are now accepted, all carry the same

Silver Egyptian Mau

Bronze Egyptian Mau

markings. A pale ground colour contrasts with the darker pattern which takes the form of random spotting on the body (which must not look as though it links into mackerel stripes), barring on the legs, a line of spots along the spine, which continues as a stripe along the length of the tail (which is ringed with a dark tip) and very specific markings on the face. The cheeks are barred with a line from the corner of the eye and another curving upward from the centre of the cheek, which meet below the base of the ear. A clear M mark on the forehead continues as frown marks between the ears.

Silver Mau has a silver ground with charcoal markings. Lips, nose and eyes are outlined in black, paw pads are black and nose leather brick red.

Bronze Mau is dark bronze on the saddle shading to creamy ivory on the belly, marked with dark brown with brown outlining, brown or black paw pads and brick nose leather.

Smoke Mau has a charcoal coat over a silver undercoat and black markings. Outlining, paw pads and nose leather are all black.

Pewter Mau is pale fawn with each hair banded silver and beige, with black tipping which diminishes towards the belly. Markings are charcoal to dark brown, outlining dark brown, leather and paw pads charcoal to dark brown, and nose leather brick red.

ORIENTAL TABBY (SPOTTED) SHORTHAIR

This British breed is very like the Mau, but it is not derived from Egyptian stock. Tabby kittens of foreign type which were produced during the breeding of the Tabby Point Siamese were used to create a new breed which looked like the ancient Egyptian cats. They are in effect a spotted Siamese and, although originally known as Egyptian Mau, when given recognition in 1978 the name was changed to Oriental Spotted. They have striped legs, a ringed tail and tabby-marked face, with the M mark on the forehead extending to form a scarab shape between the ears, lines from it running down to the shoulders.

The spots may vary in size but should be round and evenly distributed, nowhere becoming a broken mackerel stripe, not even on the spine, though the legs may be barred or spotted. The tail should have a solid tip. All except the cream and red must have

Oriental Tabby Shorthair

green eyes. This breed does not include tortoiseshells, which are grouped separately.

Brown Oriental Tabby has dense black spotting on a warm coppery brown ground of agouti fur, with black or brown paw pads, black eye rims and nose leather (or nose pink outlined in black).

Oriental Spotted Shorthairs

Cinnamon

Lilac

Red

Blue

Silver

Chocolate

Cream

Blue Oriental Tabby has light to medium blue spotting on a beige ground with blue paw pads, eye rims and nose leather (or a pink nose outlined in blue).

Chocolate Oriental Tabby has light chocolate spotting on a warm bronze ground, with chocolate paw pads, eye rims and nose leather, or pinkish brown pads and pink nose outlined in brown.

Lilac Oriental Tabby has lilac spotting on a cool beige ground, with solid faded lilac or pinkish lilac paw pads and eye rims.

Red Oriental Tabby has red spotting on a bright apricot ground with pink paw pads, nose leather pink, or pink outlined in red,warm bronze ground, with chocolate paw pads, eye rims. Eyes are copper to green, but green is preferred.

Cream Oriental Tabby has rich cream spots on a pale cream ground with solid pink paw pads, pink nose leather, or pink outlined with cream, and pink or cream eye rims. Eyes are copper to green with green preferred.

Cinnamon Oriental Shorthair has a preliminary standard of cinnamon brown spots on a burnt orange agouti ground, with tan paw pads, eye rims and nose leather, or pink nose leather outlined in tan.

Oriental Silver Spotted Tabby Preliminary standards for this cat allow all the spottings described above but on a silvery ground coat: black on silver, chocolate on a paler silver, cinammon on pale silvery cinammon, lilac on pale silvery lilac, red on pale silvery cream and cream on a silvery off-white. Leather, paw pads and eyes as described above.

ORIENTAL CLASSIC TABBY

This British breed has been given preliminary standards in all the colours described for the Oriental Spotted Tabby, with both standard and silver ground colours, but with the standard or blotched tabby pattern instead of spotting.

ORIENTAL TORTOISESHELL

Although the provisional British standard separates the tortoiseshell range it is the same in type as the other Oriental cats. It may be either black, blue, chocolate or lilac tortie, patched with red and/or cream as appropriate. Paw pads and nose leather should be patched with pink and the basic colour, eye rims pink, or matching the base colour, and eyes copper to green with green preferred.

ORIENTAL SMOKE

Also treated separately are the smoke orientals, the coats of which may be deeply tipped with any one of the colours given for the Oriental Spotted and Oriental Tortoiseshells over a near white undercoat, with the leather and eyes given for those varieties, but with eau de nil preferred where the eyes are green. Short hairs with ghost tabby markings give a watered silk affect on the body and there should be silvery frown markings on the forehead and silvery rings around the eyes.

ORIENTAL SHADED

This is another cat like the Oriental Tabby in type but with tipped fur in any of the colours previously described, over an undercoat of pale warm cream or, in silver varieties, of nearly white, which shades from dark on the top to pale below. The colour range is the same as the Oriental Smoke but not so deeply tipped.

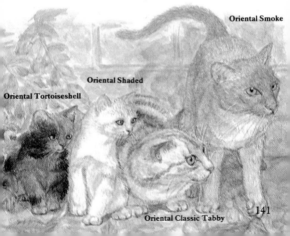

Oriental Smoke

Oriental Shaded

Oriental Tortoiseshell

Oriental Classic Tabby

141

Ocicat

OCICAT

This is an American breed, not fully recognized, which also looks like the cats in ancient Egyptian paintings, with its spotted body and tabby-marked face. Its ancestry includes Siamese and Abyssinian, since it originated in the mating of a Chocolate Point Siamese with an half-Siamese, half Abyssinian female. The name comes from its similarity in appearance to the Ocelot. It is quite a large cat when fully grown and has a short silky coat. The first to be bred were the Dark Chestnut, with chestnut brown spots on a light cream body colour, and the Light Chestnut, with chocolate brown spots, both having golden eyes. Silver and Bronze Ocicats have also been produced.

RUSSIAN BLUE

The Russian Blue is a natural breed and may be the cat which British sailors and merchants trading with the north Russian port of Archangel in the time of Elizabeth I are said to have taken home with them and called the Archangel Cat. Blue cats used to be called Maltese cats in the 17th century and that was the name by which this breed was often known in America in the early 1900s.

At least two kinds of blue cat were seen in the early British shows: the British Blue (page 68) and a foreign type variously known as the Russian, Spanish, Maltese or Archangel Cat. They both competed in the same class and the cobby British Blue almost always the found most favour. It was not until 1912 that the

Russian Blue

143

Russian (or Foreign, as it was then officially called) was given a separate class. Only one British cattery kept the breed going during World War II, though at the same time interest in the breed began in Sweden, breeding from a blue cat and a Siamese.

In Britain too, Siamese blood was introduced in re-establishing the stock after the war and, for a time, the British standard required an all Blue Siamese type cat. Then there was a return to the original type, so that on both sides of the Atlantic, a Siamese type is now undesirable.

The standards now require a cat with a long, graceful body, long legs and a long, tapering tail. In Britain the feet are small and oval, but in America more rounded. The head forms a short wedge with a flat skull and the British standard specifies prominent whisker pads. The large ears are wide at the base and have thin, translucent skin with little inside hair. In Britain they are set high on the head, but in America a less oriental position is required. The wide-set eyes are rounded in America but almond-shaped in Britain. In both cases they should be vivid green.

The fur of the Russian Blue is short, thick and very fine and the double coat makes it stand away from the body. Soft and silky, it has a distinct silvery sheen as the guard hairs are silver tipped. In America lighter shades, and in Britain a medium blue, are preferred. In America nose leather is slate grey and paw pads lavender pink or mauve, but in Britain both should be blue.

RUSSIAN WHITE

A British preliminary standard has been issued for an all white Russian cat with the same conformation and the same short, thick, silky double coat of fur. The almond-shaped eyes are green, nose leather and paw pads pink. Siamese type in this cat is undesirable.

RUSSIAN BLACK

A jet black Russian type cat has also been given a preliminary standard in Britain. In all respects, except colour, like the Russian Blue, it should have vivid green eyes and black paws and nose leather.

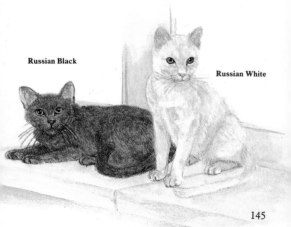

Russian Black

Russian White

ABYSSINIAN

The Abyssinian cat, like the Egyptian Mau; has been put forward as a direct descendant of the cat of the ancient Egyptians and a cat called Zulu, brought back from Ethiopia in 1868, is said to be the ancestor of the breed. It is true that it has some similarity with the cats in Egyptian art and it has the agouti coat of the African Wild Cat, which was probably one of the ancestors of the domestic cat, but a picture of Zulu published in about 1874 looks nothing like the modern cat and the agouti coat is of fairly common occurrence, being one form of the tabby. However, the breed was listed as early as 1882 and a photograph of 1903 shows a cat of the modern breed type. The Abyssinian may be a reversion to an ancient type, but it is almost certainly the creation of British breeders.

Each hair of an agouti coat is marked with two or three bands of darker colour and it is this ticking which gives the Abyssinian its distinctive fur. This is a lithe, medium-sized cat of foreign type with a firm, muscular built. The medium-long body, set on slim legs with small oval feet, carries a long and tapering tail and the broad head tapers to a firm wedge set on an elegant neck. The head has a gentle contour with a rounding to the brow and a slight nose break leading to a firm chin. The largish ears are wide set, broad based and pricked; they should be well-cupped and preferably tufted. The large eyes have an oriental setting and may be amber, hazel or green.

Around the eyes there is a line of dark pigment and dark lines run from the inner corners of the eyes up over the forehead, both edged with light-coloured fur. Darker colour extends well up the back of the hind legs and there is a solid tip of darker colour at the end of the tail, but there should be no barring or stripes elsewhere. Abyssinians tend to have white patches around the lips and lower jaw, but when this occurs it must not extend on to the neck and there must be no other white marks.

Usual Abyssinian, or **Ruddy Abyssinian**, is the original colour in this breed. It has base hair of

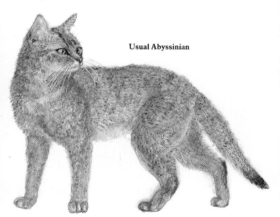

Usual Abyssinian

ruddy-orange or rich apricot, with black ticking giving an effect of rich golden brown. The belly and inside of the legs match the base hair and any shading on the spine is of a deeper colour. Markings on tail, face and hind legs are in black, as are the paw pads. The nose leather is brick red.

Blue Abyssinian, now recognized with full status in Britain, has base hair of a pale cream or oatmeal colour, with a body colour of blue grey, each hair tipped with deep steel blue. The belly and inside of the legs are pale cream or oatmeal and the face marks and dark areas on the back legs and tail are

Blue Abyssinian

Red (Sorrel) Somali

deep steel blue. The nose leather is dark pink and the pads a mauvish blue.

Red Abyssinian, also known as the **Sorrel**, is lustrous copper red, ticked with chocolate, the base hair being deep apricot. The tail tip, back of the rear legs and the face markings are chocolate. Nose leather and paw pads should be pink.

Chocolate Abyssinian, at present with only a preliminary standard in Britain, is a rich golden brown ticked with chocolate, the base hair being

149

paler, with the belly and inside of the legs the same colour and any spinal shading a darker colour. The tail tip and back of the hind legs are rich chocolate as are the pad pads, but the nose leather is pinky chocolate.

Fawn Abyssinian, a dilute form of the Sorrel, is another colour with a preliminary standard in Britain. The body colour is a warm fawn given a powdered effect by tipping with a deeper shade of the same colour. The tail tip and solid colour on the hind legs should match the spine colour, the base hair, the belly and the inside of the legs paler. Nose leather is pink and paw pads mauve-pink.

Chocolate Abyssinian

Fawn Abyssinian

Silver Abyssinian

Lilac Abyssinian

Lilac Abyssinian, also given a British preliminary standard, has a warm pinkish dove grey coat ticked with a deeper shade of the same colour. It is a dilute form of the Chocolate. Base hair, belly and the inside of the legs are a pale shade, the tail tip, hind leg solid area and any spinal shading are the same darker tone. Nose leather and paw pads are mauve-pink.

Silver Abyssinian, yet another British variety with a preliminary standard, this cat has a body colour of clear silver, ticked with black, over base hair of pale cream. Spinal shading, tail tip and the solid colour on the back of the legs are all black, belly and inside

151

Sorrel-Silver Abyssinian

Blue-Silver Abyssinian

the legs match the base hair.   Nose leather and paw pads are black.

Sorrel Silver Abyssinian The preliminary British standard describes this new variety as silvery peach, tipped chocolate, with base hair of pale cream. The dark areas are chocolate, the pale ones pale cream. Nose leather and paw pads are pink.

Blue Silver Abyssinian, The preliminary British standard describes a sparkling effect: silvery blue-grey fur ticked with deep steel blue. Base hair and pale areas cream, dark shading steel blue. Nose leather is dark pink and the paw pads mauve-blue.

BURMESE

All the Burmese breed can trace their origin back to a cat which was taken to America from Rangoon in 1930. Its actual origin is uncertain and no similar cats were then known, although some solid colour versions of the Siamese had appeared in the previous century which may actually have been the same type. Like the Siamese, Burmese carry a colour restricton but it is not so strong in its effect as that of the Siamese. Kittens show point markings very clearly, but these become less noticeable in the adult cat, although they never disappear.

That first Burmese was bred with the closest type of cat available, the Siamese, and kittens then bred back with their mother, producing in succeeding generations some cats that were pointed, some dark, still with a trace of points, and some almost solid in colour, until by 1936 they bred sufficiently true to be recognized in America as a breed. Some other cats were brought from Burma but, by the mid 1940s, so many Siamese were being used by breeders that their cats were developing strong Siamese characteristics and it was decided to suspend registration. It was at this time, just after the Second World War, that Burmese were first taken from America to Europe, where they were given recognition in 1952 by the British Cat Fancy. In France they were at first known as Zibellines. In 1953 recognition was restored in the United States, but with cats returning to the preferred type. However, British cats followed the type which had considerable Siamese blood so that the standards on opposite sides of the Atlantic now differ considerably in the type that they demand, although both require a cat which is distinctly different from the Siamese.

The British standard requires a cat that should feel hard and muscular but look lighter than it actually weighs. The back should be straight and the chest rounded, the legs slender with neat oval paws and the medium length tail straight and untapering, except near the rounded tip. The head is slightly rounded on the top, with wide cheek bones, and tapers to a short wedge. Medium large, wide-based ears have rounded tips and in profile can be seen to tilt forward. The large eyes are rounded below but their top line has a straight slant towards the nose. Both round and oriental eyes are considered a fault. The very glossy coat is short and fine and lies close to the body. The American standards differ in asking for a rounded head, without flat planes, and a visible nose break. They require round eyes and round paws. In Britain eyes may be any shade of yellow from chartreuse to amber, with golden yellow preferred, but in America they may range only from yellow to gold, with the deepest and most brilliant preferred.

The Cat Fanciers Association, in the United States, accepts only the Brown, or Sable Burmese and calls the more recent colours Malayan cats.

Like the Siamese, Burmese cats are very affectionate and become attached to people, liking to share human activity. The males, as well as females, usually

154

Brown Burmese

make very attentive parents. Burmese have a reputation for wandering rather widely, and for being hunters able to deal with quite large prey. Although they are people-cats they are not ideal for keeping entirely indoors.

Brown (or Sable) Burmese were the original variety, they should have a coat of rich, warm sable brown fur (seal brown, the British standard calls it) which shades almost imperceptibly to a lighter tone on the underparts. The fur is fine and short, its silky texture producing a distinctly glossy coat. The British standard allows slightly darker ears and mask. Nose leather and paw pads are brown. Eyes may be yellow to gold in America and yellow to chartreuse or amber in Britain, though a golden yellow is preferred. In a Brown Burmese green eyes would be considered a fault, but faint tabby markings are not a disqualification in kittens and very young cats.

155

Blue Burmese/Blue Malayan

Blue Burmese (Blue Malayan) gained breed status in Britain in the 1960s and is now recognized by several North American cat associations. The British standard specifies a coat of soft silvery grey only very slightly darker on the back and tail. Rounded areas, such as ears, face and feet, should have a distinct silver sheen. Paw pads should be grey and nose leather very dark grey. In America a darker cat is preferred, having a rich blue coat with fawn seasonal overtones. Paw pads and nose leather are slate grey with a pinkish tinge.

Lilac Burmese, recognized in Britain, have a coat of delicate dove grey with a slightly pinkish cast. Ears and mask may be slightly darker. Nose leather and paw pads are shell pink in kittens but become lavender pink as they mature.

Chocolate Burmese, the British variety originating in the American Champagne, should have fur the colour of milk chocolate, according to the standard, and the ideal coat has the same warm even colour throughout, although the ears and mask may be slightly darker, provided that the legs, tail and lower jaw are the same colour as the back. Nose leather should be chocolate brown and the paw pads brick pink shading to chocolate.

Chocolate Burmese

Lilac Burmese

Red Burmese, a variety recognized in Britain, has a coat of light tangerine colour. As in all red cats, tabby markings tend to occur and are permissible on the face, and indeterminate markings elsewhere (except the sides and belly), provided that the cat is excellent in other ways. The ears should be distinctly darker than the back. Nose leather and paw pads are pink.

Cream Burmese, another variety recognized in Britain, has a rich cream coat when adult, with ears only slightly darker than the colour of the back. As in the red, slight tabby markings are not considered a fault in an otherwise good cat. Nose leather and paw pads are pink.

Platinum Burmese (Platinum Malayan) are the equivalent of Lilac in the United States, but their coat is described as silvery-grey with seasonal fawn overtones. Paw pads and nose leather are lavender pink.

Cream Burmese

Champagne Burmese (Champagne Malayan) is the American dilute form of the Sable which, when adult, should have a coat of rich, warm honey-beige, shading to a lighter tone on the chest, belly and the inside of the legs, darker shading on the face and ears being permitted. The nose leather should be a light warm brown and the paw pads pinkish.

**Champagne Burmese
Champagne Malayan
(American type)**

Red Burmese

159

Tortoiseshell Burmese are known in Britain in all the possible forms: Brown Tortie, Blue Tortie (Blue Cream), Chocolate Tortie and Lilac Tortie. However, these cats do not have black fur, which is already dilute in the Brown, so that they have bi-colour rather than tri-colour coats:

Brown Tortie Burmese

Chocolate Tortie Burmese

Lilac Tortie Burmese

160

Blue Tortie Burmese

Brown Tortie has brown and red fur with no obvious marking. Its nose leather and paw pads may be plain or blotched brown and pink.

Blue Tortie (Blue Cream) has a mixture of blue and cream fur with nose leather and paw pads plain or blotched in blue and pink.

Chocolate Tortie has a mixture of chocolate and red fur with nose leather and paw pads plain or blotched in chocolate and pink.

Lilac Tortie has a coat of mixed lilac and cream with nose leather and paw pads plain or blotched lilac and pink.

161

TONKINESE

This American breed was produced by crossing the
Burmese with the Siamese. The British Burmese is
too like the Siamese in type to produce an hybrid that
would be noticeably different, but this was possible
with the differences found in the American Burmese
type. The result is a medium-sized cat which has a
head of slightly rounded wedge shape. The tail tapers
to a point and the feet are neat and oval. The muzzle
is rather square and there is a rise from the bridge of
the nose to the forehead. The medium-sized ears tilt
slightly forwards and have rounded tips. The eyes are
almond-shaped and have a slightly oriental slant.
They are a rich blue-green in colour.

Unlike the Burmese, in which the Siamese points
and mask are not intended to be noticeable, the
Tonkinese retains them clearly as areas of darker fur,
but with the edges softened and merging into the
body colour. Several coat colours have been bred.

Natural Mink Tonkinese has a warm brown coat
with points and mask of darker brown, ranging from
sable to chocolate.

Honey Mink Tonkinese has a coat of a more reddish
brown and reddish points.
Other colours of Tonkinese which have been produced are Champagne, Blue and Chocolate, the main
colour being as in the Burmese, with appropriately
darker markings.

Honey Mink Tonkinese

Natural Mink Tonkinese

163

KORAT

This is another cat from Thailand and has been known for centuries in the region of the Korat Plateau, where they are held to bring good luck. A similar silver-blue cat is illustrated in *The Cat Book Poems* from Ayudha (see page 112) and described by one poet as having

'hairs so smooth, with tips like clouds and roots like silver;
with eyes that shine like dewdrops on a lotus leaf'

The Korat is indeed a beautiful silver blue, with single tipping that develops through kittenhood until complete at about two years old. Short to medium in length, it is fine and close-lying, sometimes parting over the spine as the cat moves.

Korat

The medium-sized body is strong, muscular and semi-cobby, with a medium-length tail, heavy at the base and tapering to a rounded tip. The head is heart-shaped with a large flat forehead and a gentle curve to the muzzle, which is neither square nor sharply pointed. Large ears are set high on the head and round tipped, and the nose is short with a slight stop between it and the forehead. The eyes are disproportionally large and are fully round when open, but have an oriental slant when partly closed. They are a brilliant green, but this develops with adulthood and kittens have yellow or amber eyes. Nose leather and lips are dark blue or lavender and the pads on the oval paws range from dark blue to lavender with a pinkish tinge.

The first Korat seen in a show was probably one brought from Thailand and entered as a Siamese in a National Cat Club Show at Holland House in 1896: it was disqualified by the judge. Many years later, in 1959, a pair from Bangkok were registered in the United States, the breed first gaining recognition there in 1966. Korats officially reached Britain in 1972 and gained recognition in 1975.

In their homeland Korat males are known as tough fighters but they also are said to make gentle fathers and females are ideal mothers. They are said to retain their vitality and playfulness throughout their lives and, like the Siamese, do not like being left out of anything. Unlike the Siamese, they have rather quiet voices.

JAPANESE BOBTAIL

The Japanese Bobtail is a naturally occurring breed
which has been known in Japan for centuries and can
also be found in China and Korea. It does not fit into
any of the other shorthair categories, for it is not like
any other kind of cat. The most immediately noticeable difference is the short bobbed tail from which it
gets its western name. The cat's overall build is of
basically foreign (oriental) type, well muscled but
straight and slender with long clean lines. However,
the head is quite different from other foreign breeds ,
for the cheek bones are very high and the nose long
and parallel, with the eyes set at a pronounced slant
when viewed from the side.

Cats of this type can be seen in the paintings and
woodblock prints of the Japanese masters such as
Ando Hiroshige and Ichiyussi Kuniyoshi, along with
other cats with tails. They do not appear to have been
particularly remarked upon and, even when an
interest in cats and pedigree breeds developed in
Japan after World War II, little interest was shown in
them until visiting American judges expressed their
admiration for the Bobtail in 1963. Yet the Bobtail
had been the traditional form of the *Maneki-Neko*, the
figure of a beckoning cat, which appears in shop
doorways to welcome customers or is kept in homes
as an ornament and a good luck symbol. It appears on
the facade of the Gotokuji temple in Tokyo and is
shown asleep in a celebrated life-like carving over the
entrance to the shrine at Toshogu.

Japanese Bobtail

The favourite colours in Japan are those of the Tortoiseshell and White, or Calico cat: red, black and white, known as the *mi-ke*, for the tri-colour is considered particularly lucky. Like all tortoiseshells it is usually female.

The American standards, in addition to the features described above, ask for a medium-sized cat, with a long but shapely body and long slender legs with oval paws. The hind legs are longer than the forelegs but kept angled when the cat is relaxed so that the body remains level. The legs should not be dainty in

Japanese Bobtails

appearance. The ears are large and set wide apart and at right angles to the head, so that they have the appearance of being titled forward, and the large, rather oval, eyes have a shallow curvature to the eyeball so that they do not give the impression of bulging beyond the cheekbone, desite their angle.

The bobbed tail is actually about 12cm (5in) long, but bends forwards to give the impression of a length of only about half this much. The tail fur should be rather longer and thicker hair than that on the rest of

168

the body, so that it looks like a pompom or the tail of a rabbit set on the end of the spine, camouflaging its real shape. The rest of the cat's coat is of medium length and soft and silky, with no noticeable undercoat.

The Japanese Bobtail has been recognized in all colours and patterns except for the agouti coat of the Abyssinian and the pointed pattern of the Siamese but *mi-ke* cats are preferred and other black, red and white cats are favoured in breeding lines to help produce them. In bi-colours and tri-colours any colour maybe predominant and preference is given to vivid contrast and bold markings. Nose leather, pawpads and eye colour should match the coat colours as specified for other short-haired cats.

Mi-ke Japanese Bobtail

SNOW SHOE CAT

This variety, also sometimes known as Silver Laces, was developed by North American breeders to transfer the white-pawed, pointed pattern of the Birman (see page 222) to a short-haired cat. The result is a breed with a head rather longer in type than in the Birman, though not so long as in the Siamese, and with a short coat which may be any of the colours accepted for the Birman. It has been recognized by only a few cat associations in the United States and is not known in Britain.

Snowshoe Cat

Long-haired Cats

Angora

ANGORA (TURKISH ANGORA)

The Angora was possibly the first kind of long-haired cat known in Europe and America, being taken to France and England in the 16th century, but the cat fanciers of the 19th century preferred the Persian type of long-haired cat and Angoras disappeared from the breeds known outside their native Turkey. Their name comes from that of the Turkish capital, Ankara, where they survived only because of a deliberate breeding programme at Ankara Zoo. In 1963 animals from the zoo were taken to America to revive the breed and later Angoras also reached Britain.

The American Turkish Angora was developed as a pure white cat, but in its native land the Angora is known in many colours including the *Sarman* (Red Tabby), *Teku* (Silver Tabby) and *Ankara kedi* (Ankara Cat, an odd-eyed white), and since 1978 a wide range of colours has been recognized by the American cat associations.

In Britain the breed was recreated by a careful breeding programme, rather than by imports from Turkey, but an identical cat has been evolved – except that, since it was developed partly from Siamese, it has a harsher voice, more like that breed.

The Angora is a small to medium-size cat, the male slightly bigger than the female, with a sturdy body that is long and graceful and carried on long legs with small round paws. The rump is slightly high because the hind legs are longer than the front. The tail is long and tapering, wide at the base and often carried curled forward over the body. The head is wedge-shaped, with long, wide-spaced, pointed ears set high upon the head, and large almond-shaped eyes, though they are more round than oriental. The nose has no break, the chin is rounded and the neck is slim and fairly long.

The silky fur of the Angora is medium-long on the body and very long on the ruff, with a full, feathery tail that tends to waves.

The British preliminary standard recognizes all the colours accepted in Foreign Shorthairs: black, white (with either blue, orange, odd or green eyes), blue, chocolate, lilac, red, tortie, cream, blue tortie, chocolate tortie, lilac tortie and tabby in all these colours. Eye colour follows that for other longhairs.

Angora

TURKISH (TURKISH VAN)

This is another long-established type of cat in its native Turkey but it was almost unknown elsewhere until a British breeder, undismayed by quarantine regulations, imported a breeding pair into Britain in 1955. In 1969 they were recognized as a breed and have now been taken to the United States.

The Turkish Cat, was first known in Britain as the Turkish Van Cat, and it comes from the area of south-eastern Turkey near Lake Van. It has been nicknamed the 'swimming cat' because it appears to enjoy being in water and will take to a stream back home. (Angoras are also said to like water.) On a hot sunny day they can be left to dry off after swimming or bathing but otherwise they should be dried rapidly with a warm towel, according to their original British breeder. Nevertheless, they are hardy animals – around Lake Van there may be snow for six months of the year.

The Turkish Cat is similar to the Angora, but less foreign looking and of a more sturdy stature: the body long, the legs of medium length with neat round feet, the tail of medium length and the males particularly muscular on the neck and shoulders. The head is a short wedge, wider and shorter than that of the Angora, but with a longish nose and with smaller, upright ears, set fairly close together, and round eyes.

The coat of the Turkish cat should be long, soft and silky to the roots and with no woolly undercoat. There are tufts of fur between the toes, tufted ears, a substantial ruff and a full feathery tail. The British standard follows the pattern of native Van Cats and requires a chalk white coat with no trace of yellow, marked with auburn on the face but leaving a white blaze and with the ears white. The tail is also auburn and in kittens may have distinct ring markings, but these should become quite faint in the adult cat. Kittens have their auburn colour patches from birth but take a long time to develop the luxuriant adult coat. The nose leather, paw pads and the inside of the

Turkish (Turkish Van)

ears should be a delicate shell pink and the eyes a light amber with their rims pink-skinned. Some cats have small auburn markings irregularly placed on the body which do not disqualify otherwise good specimens.

Some American cat bodies recognize this cat under the original name of Turkish Van and require similar auburn patching on white fur. Like the Angora, the Turkish or Van cat is a natural breed, not a human creation and though in Britain the Angora is something of a recreation, the Turkish has been developed by direct descent from from imported cats.

Turkish Van - 'the swimming cat'

MAINE COON CAT

Since the mid-19th century at least, and possibly for much longer, the Maine Coon Cat has been an established breed in the State of Maine, where it was known as a hardy working cat, able to withstand the tough winters. Its name comes from the idea that it is the result of matings between domestic cats and racoons, but that would be impossible, and it is probably the result of crosses between domestic shorthaired cats, introduced by early settlers, and Angoras taken across the Atlantic by later seafarers. The first registered individual was a black and white recorded in 1861 and right through the rest of the 19th century it was a popular cat. These cats were shown even before cat shows became a regular event. However, their popularity waned until revived after the founding of the Central Maine Coon Cat Club in 1953, and in 1967 a standard was drawn up and the breed then gained modern recognition.

Maine Coons can be big animals, weighing as much as 13.5 kilos (30lbs), and muscular, but they have the long-bodied, long-legged look of the Angora with a small to medium, tapering head. The cheek bones are set high, the chin is in line with the nose and upper lip, the large eyes are slightly slanting and the large ears are set high on the head. The paws are large and round and the tail long, wide at the base and tapering.

The coat is heavy and shaggy, though not so long as in the Persian cats, nor with such a heavy ruff, although a frontal ruff is desirable. There are tufts of

Maine Coon Cat

fur between the toes and the ears are well tufted too.
Fur may be black, white, red or cream solid colour,
the whole range of tabbies, tipped coats and parti-
colour coats and tabby with white, which should
appear on the bib, belly and all four paws to match
the Cat Fanciers Association standard. Eyes may be
green, gold or copper and, in white cats, blue or
odd-eyed also.

NORWEGIAN FOREST CAT

The Norsk Skaukatt, as it is known in its native country, is a natural breed which is found in Scandinavia. It is somewhat like the Maine Coon Cat in appearance and has developed the same tough constitution. It differs from the Maine Coon in that its back legs must be longer than the forelegs and it must have a double coat. The woolly undercoat and medium-length topcoat keep it warm in the northern winter and protect it from the weather. It was developed as a pedigree breed from indigenous feral and farm cats in the 1930s but the type had been long established and makes its appearance in local fairy tales. All colours are permitted.

Norwegian Forest Cat

LONGHAIRS (PERSIANS)

The Angora was not the only long-haired cat to appear in Renaissance Europe, another, more chunky cat arrived about the same date, possibly taken back by travellers and merchants from what is now Iran. It subsequently became known as the Persian cat, although in Britain the official name is now simply Longhair. At the cat shows of the late 19th century the Persian was taken up as the fashionable cat and emphasis placed upon the features which are now characteristic of most modern long-haired pedigree cats. These cats have cobby bodies – deep in the chest and massive across the shoulders and the rump, the body overall short well-rounded and low lying – with short, sturdy legs having large, round paws with the toes close together. Their tails are short and carried without a curve and usually at an angle lower than the back. The round and massive head has a wide skull and a short, broad snub nose with a clear 'break' where it is angled from the head. The large eyes are very round and set well apart. The ears are small, round-tipped and tilted forward, not very open at the base. They are far apart and low on the head so that they do not noticeably interrupt its rounded contour. In all these features American cats tend to be of a more extreme type than the British. There they are officially known as Persians, a name still often used in Britain, despite the official designation 'Longhair.'

The Longhair or Persian cat's coat should be long and thick, standing off from the body but fine and silky in texture, never woolly. It should be long all over the body, with a big ruff, which continues in a deep frill between the front legs, and luxuriant fur on the tail. There are long tufts in the ears and between the toes.

In America all the colour forms share a single standard but in Britain they are classified separately (as given here). Though they share the same ideal conformation some colours seem to achieve it more closely than others, solid colour blues and blacks generally coming closest to the standard.

There are two colours – the solid colour lilac and chocolate – that are not recognized within the Persian group by some American bodies, but are given the name Kashmirs and grouped with the Himalayans.

Black Longhair (Black Persian) This was actually the first pedigree breed to be recognized in Britain (it is numbered Variety 1). It should have a lustrous, raven black coat with the fur free of any tinge of

Black Longhair/Black Persian

181

White Longhair/White Persian

rustiness and no sign of a single white hair. Kittens are born with black fur but it frequently loses its blackness, looking greyish or rusty, but regaining its coal black colour as the cat becomes adult. However, too much lying in the sun or dampness can affect the coat colour and should be avoided if you intend to show the cat. The nose leather and paw pads should be black and the eyes copper or deep orange.

White Longhair (White Persian) This variety may have orange or blue eyes or one of each: blue-eyed whites having the possibility of deafness (see page 71), though not all whites with blue eyes are deaf and

sometimes orange-eyed whites suffer this affliction. White Longhairs have a pure, glistening white coat. Their nose leather and paw pads are pink. If odd-eyed the eyes should have an equal depth of colour.

Although white cats seem to be fastidious about keeping clean, their paws and feet cannot avoid getting dirty and may require washing if being shown. Wiping the feet after a cat has been out will help to stop dirt from building up. Grease stains can be minimized by dusting with talcum powder when grooming, to absorb the grease, and the corners of the eyes must be kept clean to avoid staining on the face.

Blue Longhair (Blue Persian) A lighter shade of blue is preferred in American Persian cats, provided that the colour is even from head to tail and sound to the roots – a darker a shade is preferable to uneven colour. In Britain any shade is allowable in the Blue Longhair, provided it is even and free of markings or white hairs. The nose leather and paw pads should be blue and the eyes brilliant copper or deep orange. Kittens which have faint tabby markings at birth usually lose them as they grow older.

Red Longhair (Red Persian) As in the short-haired red cats, the tabby markings are difficult to lose in Red Longhairs but the longer fur tends to break up the pattern so that the markings are less noticeable. However, cats which perfectly match the description of the standards on both sides of the Atlantic that there shall be no markings, are rare. The colour should be a deep rich red. Red Self and Red Tabby cats can appear in the same litter so that it is difficult to know whether a tabby marked kitten will lose its marks. Nose leather and paw pads should be brick red and the eyes a deep copper in colour.

Cream Longhair (Cream Persian) Very careful breeding has created a Cream Longhair coat that is free of tabby markings, despite the fact that cream is a dilute form of red, in which the tabby pattern is so

**Red Longhair/
Red Persian**

Blue Longhair/Blue Persian

185

Cream

Lilac

Chocolate

186

predominant. The Cream Persian had its origin in a fawn variety of the early Angoras, but the modern cat is probably more the result of matings between reds and blues and perhaps from very pale reds. Breeding from Cream to Cream leads to loss of type, both in conformation and in the development of a hot reddish tone along the backbone. Cross-breeding with Blues helps to correct this in succeeding generations. The Cream Longhair has pink nose leather and paw pads and bright copper or orange eyes.

Chocolate Longhair (Brown Persian) Also known in the United States as the Solid Brown Himalayan and the Brown Kashmir, this cat was created only after the development of the Colourpoints (Himalayans in America), in which some solid-colour chocolate cats appeared in the same litters as the chocolate points. This is why some associations still class them with the Himalayans or Kashmirs. In the early days of the variety the fur was frequently found to fade or bleach and it has taken a long time to produce a coat of sound and even colour of the requisite medium to dark chocolate brown. The nose leather and paw pads match the fur and the eyes are deep orange or copper.

Lilac Longhair (Lavender Persian) Blue cats were used in the breeding programme to produce the Chocolate Persian and this produced some solid-colour lilac cats. The British standard requires a pinkish dove grey coat with matching leather and orange eyes.

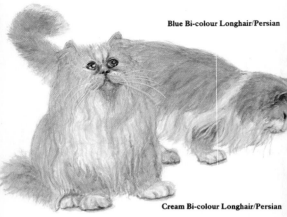

Blue Bi-colour Longhair/Persian

Cream Bi-colour Longhair/Persian

Bi-colour Longhairs (Parti-color Persians) When first given recognition in Britain the Bi-colour had to be a cat of solid colour and white, with the white areas confined to the underparts, except for the face which was divided neatly in half. This proved too difficult to achieve and in 1977 was amended to permit a much less formal distribution of any solid colour on white, although the original 'Dutch' pattern is still admired. In both Britain and America either black, blue, red or cream patching is accepted, with an inverted V blaze on the face being desirable. Nose leather and paw pads match the coat colours and eyes should be copper or orange.

Black Bi-colour Longhair/Persian

Red Bi-colour Longhair/Persian

189

Persian Van Bi-color This variation on the Bicolor, recognized in America, has patching on the head and tail as in the Turkish Van (see page 174). Ideally the body should be clear of colour, but in practice one or two patches are permitted.

Tortoiseshell Longhair (Tortoiseshell Persian) The three colours of the tortoiseshell coat: red, black and cream, should be rich and bright in colour and well broken into clearly defined patches all over, with only slightly less patching on the legs and face, even the ears carrying broken colour. The American standard says a cream or red blaze on the face is desirable and although not mentioned in the British standard it is preferred. Long fur softens even the crispest patched markings which become diffused. The CFA actually describes this as a black cat with patches of red and cream but the coat should not be predominantly black. Nose leather and paw pads can be pink or black and eyes are brilliant copper or deep orange. Tortoiseshells are almost always female.

Blue Cream Longhair (Blue Cream Persian) Created originally from Blue and Cream cross-breeding, the Blue Cream is a dilute form of Tortoiseshell. In America clearly defined patching is required, and the CFA standard describes this as a blue cat with patches of solid cream, but the British standard requires a soft intermingling of the colours. Thus a prize British cat would be penalized on the American show bench and vice-versa. Nose leather and paw pads are pink and blue and eyes copper or deep orange.

Tortoiseshell Longhair/ Persian

Blue Cream Longhair/ Persian

Chocolate Tortoiseshell Longhair A recent British variety in which the black ground is replaced by a chocolate brown and patched with red and cream. the eyes are deep orange or copper. Nose leather and paw pads may be pink or brown.

Lilac Cream Tortoiseshell has preliminary recognition in Britain with the colours softly intermingled and pale orange or copper eyes.

Shell Tortoiseshell Persian It is only the tipping of this cat that carries the tortoiseshell colours and pattern. Like the Chinchilla and the tipped cats that follow, it has a white undercoat with the hairs of the topcoat coloured at the tips but white along most of their length to the roots. In this case the tipping is in black with well defined patches of red and cream, the three colours extending over the back, flanks, head and tail. Face and legs also carry light shading, but chin, ear tufts, stomach and chest are white or only very slightly tipped. The eyes are brilliant copper. This variety is recognized in America but not in Britain.

Shaded Tortoiseshell Persian This American variety is a darker version of the Shell Tortoiseshell Persian. A blaze of red or cream tipping is desirable on the face. The eyes are brilliant copper.

Smoke Tortoiseshell Persian The darkest of the American tortoiseshell-tipped cats, this variety has deep tipping of black, with clearly defined patches of red and cream which in repose gives it the appearance of a full tortoiseshell, but in motion allows the white undercoat to show through clearly. On the face and ears only a narrow band of white remains at the roots, which can be seen only when the fur is parted, but the ear tufts and ruff are white. A blaze of cream or red

Lilac Cream Longhair

Chocolate Tortoiseshell Longhair

Shell Tortoiseshell Persian

Smoke Tortoiseshell Persian

193

Tortoiseshell and White Longhair/Persian

Smoke Tortoiseshell Persian

tipping is desirable on the face. The eyes are brilliant copper.

Tortoiseshell and White Longhair (Tortoiseshell and White Persian) The British standard for this cat requires a tri-colour coat that is interspersed with white, rather than having the upperparts coloured and the underparts white as in the shorthair, but some American standards ask for a pattern like the shorthair with white feet, legs and underparts and splashes of white on the nose and around the neck. In some American associations the Calico is the same as the British Tortoiseshell and White. Nose leather and paw pads should carry broken colour and the eyes should be deep orange or copper.

Calico Persian Either a white cat patched with red and black or patched with red, black and cream, this is sometimes the name of the American equivalent of the British Tortoiseshell and White and in some associations a distinct separate variety, carrying more white in the coat, which predominates on the underparts. Nose leather and paw pads are pink or broken and eyes copper or deep orange.

Dilute Calico Persian This blue and cream patched cat is similar in all respects to the Calico Persian except for the softer dilute colours.

Calico Persian

Dilute Calico Persian

Chocolate Tortoiseshell and White Longhair, for which there is a British preliminary standard has, chocolate instead of black, mingled with light and dark red and interspersed with white.

Lilac Tortoiseshell and White, also given preliminary recognition, is a dilute version with lilac and cream interspersed with white.

Tabby Longhairs (Tabby Persians) Long fur tends to diffuse the edges of tabby markings, giving a softer look than in shorthairs, but smudged markings or brindling should not occur. Kittens with faint markings are not likely to develop good ones but dark kittens can often grow up to be beautifully marked cats.

Lilac Tortie and White Longhair

Chocolate Tortie and White Longhair

Silver Tabby Longhair/Persian

Brown Tabby Longhair (Brown Tabby Persian) is brilliant copper brown marked with dense black, with the back of the back leg black from paw to heel. Nose leather is brick red, paw pads are brown or black and eyes may be hazel or copper.

Silver Tabby Longhair (Silver Tabby Persian) has dense black markings on a silver ground. Nose leather is brick red, paw pads are black and eyes green or hazel.

197

Cream Tabby Longhair/Persian

Blue Tabby Persian

Cameo Tabby Longhair/Persian

Red Tabby Longhair (Red Tabby Persian) has deep red markings on a red ground, brick red nose leather, pink paw pads and copper or orange eyes.

Cream Tabby Persian This American variety has a ground colour of pale cream, including the lips and chin, which is marked with a darker buff or cream, still within the dilute colour range. Nose leather and paw pads are rose pink and the eyes brilliant copper.

Blue Tabby Persian Blue tabbies were seen in early British cat shows but this variety is not now recognized in Britain. American standards call for a pale bluish ivory coat marked with very deep blue with a warm fawn tone over all. Nose leather and paw pads are rose and eyes brilliant copper.

Cameo Tabby Persian, another American only variety, has off-white fur marked with red. Nose leather and paw pads are rose, the eyes brilliant copper.

Red Tabby Longhair/Persian

Patched Tabby Persian (Torbie Persian) This American variety is a silver, brown or blue tabby with with extra patching of red and/or cream for the brown and of just cream for the blue. Nose leather and eyes are as for the standard tabbies.

Chocolate Tabby Longhair has preliminary recognition in Britain with rich chocolate markings on a bronze agouti ground. Nose leather is chocolate or pink rimmed with chocolate, with paw pads and eye rims chocolate and eyes hazel or copper.

Lilac Tabby Longhair, another variety given preliminary recognition in Britain, has lilac markings on a beige agouti ground. Nose leather, paw pads and eye rims are faded lilac, or the nose may be pink outlined in lilac. Eyes hazel or copper. The preliminary standards for this and the Chocolate Tabby specify a spotted abdomen.

Smoke Longhair (Black Smoke Persian) 'A cat of contrasts', as the British standard describes it, the smoke has an undercoat as ash-white as possible, with the tips of the fur shading to black. The dark hair should be most apparent on the back, head and feet, with light points on the frill, flanks and ear tufts; that on the face and paws should be dark to the roots. The nose leather and paw pads are black and the eyes orange or copper. Apart from the silver ruff and ear tufts, the cat appears black when it is still, but the undercoat is revealed when the cat moves. Smoke

Chocolate Tabby Longhair

Lilac Tabby Longhair

Patched Tabby
Persian

20

Persians have been admired and shown as a separate variety since the early 1890s, but they have never been very common. Kittens often look like solid blacks and show no trace of the white undercoat, except for tiny smudges of white around the eyes or a grey tone on the stomach, and it takes many months for the contrasting coat to develop.

Blue Smoke Longhair (Blue Smoke Persian) This variety is identical to the Black Smoke in every detail except its slightly diluted colour, giving the impression of a solid blue cat when still, apart from the ruff and ear tufts. The face and paws have hair blue to the roots, the sides and flanks have tips shading to blue, the frill and ear tufts are silver and the undercoat as near white as possible. Nose leather and paw pads are blue and the eyes brilliant copper.

Chocolate Smoke Longhair has been given preliminary recognition in Britain. Over an undercoat as near white as possible its body fur shades from chocolate to silver on the sides and flanks, with mask and feet unmarked chocolate and frill and ear tufts silver. The large eyes are copper or orange.

Lilac Smoke Longhair is another variety given British preliminary recognition. The requirements follow those for the Chocolate, except that the the topcoat colour is lilac which is most clearly defined on the back, head and feet.

Chinchilla Longhair (Chinchilla Persian) One of the most striking cats in appearance, the Chinchilla has

Longhairs/Persians

Lilac Smoke

Red Smoke

Blue Smoke

Black Smoke

203

a pure white undercoat with a long, silky topcoat which is tipped with black on the back, flanks, tail, head and ears, giving it a sparkling look which has earned it the name Silver Persian, by which it is sometimes known in America. The early Chinchillas were much darker than the cats of today, some of them had a lavender colour and the early British standard required a lavender tint. Now the different colours and degrees of tipping have been separated into different varieties. The modern Chinchilla should be pure white on the chest, stomach, chin and ear tufts; the legs may be slightly shaded by tipping and the rest of the coat evenly tipped. The large round eyes are emerald or blue-green and are outlined by dark brown or black skin. Nose leather and paw pads are black or brown.

Chinchilla Golden (Golden Persian) The golden form is tipped in the same way as the Chinchilla but has an undercoat which in America is described as rich warm cream and a top coat that is tipped with seal brown, the tipping appearing on the back, flanks, head and tail and continuing as slight shading on the legs to give the overall golden appearance. The preliminary British standard is similar but describes the undercoat as apricot deepening to gold; tipping, lips, eye rims and outlines to the nose as seal or black. The chest, stomach, chin and ear tufts match the undercoat. The nose leather is deep rose in America, brick red in Britain, and the paw pads match the tipping. The eyes are green or blue-green.

Shaded Silver Persian This cat is exactly like the Chinchilla except that the tipping of the fur is heavier, giving a rather darker look. Both can appear in the

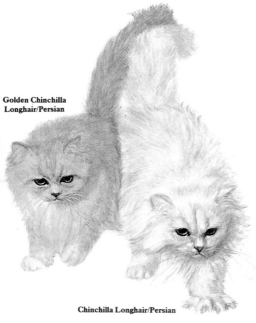

Golden Chinchilla Longhair/Persian

Chinchilla Longhair/Persian

same litter – and the darkest kittens sometimes grow up with the palest coats. In Britain, the difficulty of assigning a cat to Chinchilla or Shaded Silver led to dropping recognition of this breed. The Shaded Silver has brick red nose leather, black paw pads and lips and black outlining to the eyes and nose. The eyes are green or blue-green.

Pewter Longhair This is the modern British equivalent to the Shaded Silver, but the eyes are copper or orange with a black rim. They have a white undercoat and even black shading, giving the appearance of a pewter mantle. Nose leather is brick red and paw pads, lips and the outlining of the nose are black or dark brown.

Shaded Golden Persian has undercoat of rich cream covered by a mantle with seal brown tipping shading from dark on the face, tail and ridge of the back to cream on the chin, chest, stomach and under the tail.

Pewter Longhair

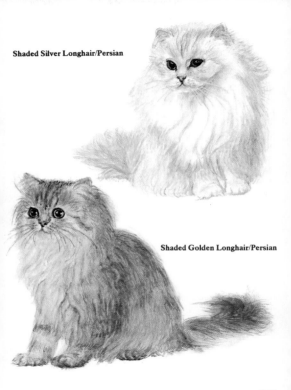

Shaded Silver Longhair/Persian

Shaded Golden Longhair/Persian

207

The effect is much darker than in the Chinchilla Golden. Legs should be the same tone as the face. Paw pads and lips are seal brown, which also outlines the green or green-blue eyes and the deep rose nose.

Shell Cameo Longhair (Shell Cameo Persian) The Cameo range of cats are the red equivalent of the black-tipped silvers. The Shell Cameo has the lightest tipping. Over a white undercoat the back, flanks, head and tail are sufficiently tipped with red to give the fur a characteristic rosy sparkle. The British standard describes it as sparkling silver dusted with rose pink. Chin, ear tufts, stomach and chest are untipped and the face and legs only lightly shaded. The nose leather, paw pads and the rims of the eyes are rose coloured and the eyes a brilliant copper. A green rim to the eye is a fault.

Shaded Cameo Longhair (Shaded Cameo Persian or Red Shaded Persian) This is the next darkest of the red-tipped cats, the general effect being of much deeper tipping than in the Shell Cameo. It ranges from dark on the back, face and tail, shading down the sides, to white on the chin, chest, stomach and under the tail. The legs should match the face. The British standard describes the effect as of a red mantle. Nose leather, paw pads and eye rims are rose and the eyes a brilliant copper.

Cameo Red Persian (Red Smoke Persian) The red tipping on this cat is so deep that in repose it appears

Shell Cameo Longhair/Persian

Shaded Cameo Longhair/Persian

Cameo Red Persian

209

a solid red, except for its white frill and ear tufts, only movement revealing the white undercoat. Nose leather, paw pads and eye rims are rose, the eyes a brilliant copper.

Tortie Cameo Longhair is recognized as a breed in Britain, it is accepted with tipping of any intensity, comparable to the three American varieties of tortoiseshell tipped cats described on pages 192-3.

Shell Cream Cameo Longhair/Persian

Cream Smoke Cameo Longhair-Persian

Cameo Cream Longhairs These are cameo cats tipped with cream, not red and are recognized in Britain in *Shell*, with a sparkling silver appearance, lightly dusted with cream, *Shaded*, slightly darker giving a cream mantle, *Cream Smoke*, which is a little darker still but shading to white on the flanks and with white frill and ear tufts, and a *Blue Cream Cameo* which has softly intermingled tipping in both colours and can be of any depth of colour. They have pink nose leather and pads, except the Blue cream which may have blue, or a mixture, and all have deep orange or copper eyes.

Shaded Cream Cameo Longhair/Persian

Blue Cream Cameo Longhair/Persian

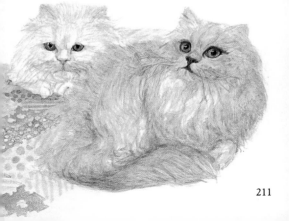

211

Peke-faced Persian An extreme form of the Persian type, this is a cat in which the face is even more flattened and the head should as closely as possible resemble that of the Pekinese dog, from which it borrows its name. The nose should be very short and depressed, even indented between the eyes, which are very large, round, set wide apart and prominent. There should be a decidedly wrinkled muzzle. The type is considered far too extreme in Britain, where there has been much concern that such bracephalic faces develop breathing difficulties (as do Pug and Pekinese dogs) or suffer from blockages or distortions of the tear ducts which drain the eyes into the nose. Another problem is that the teeth of the upper jaw may not fit against the lower jaw.

To avoid health problems the breeders have to be very selective and aim for a nose that is still long enough for proper respiration and skin folding that does not cause blocked tear ducts. This type of face can appear in normal litters and mating with a Peke-faced does not always ensure offspring of this type. Kittens may show the characteristic break between nose and forehead soon after birth, others do not develop it for as long as six months. Only two coats are recognized: the Red Tabby and the Red. Both conform to the descriptions of the Persian equivalent in all except the extreme face.

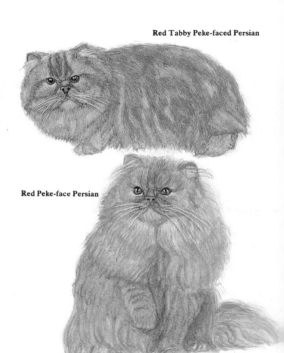

Red Tabby Peke-faced Persian

Red Peke-face Persian

213

COLOURPOINT LONGHAIRS
(HIMALAYANS)

Known as Himalayans in America and Colourpoints in Britain (not to be confused with the American Colorpoints), these are cats of full longhair or Persian type, but with the pointed pattern of the Siamese. Attempts to produce a cat of this type were begun in Sweden in the 1920s and in America in 1924 some cats like this appeared and were given the name Malayan Persians, but it was not until after World War II that a careful breeding programme in Britain produced a cat with full coat, correct longhair conformation and Siamese colouring. In 1955 they were recognized and a standard approved in Britain under the name Colourpoint Longhair. At the same time an American breeding programme produced similar cats which were given the name Himalayan and received recognition in 1957.

The problems in producing such cats lie in that if long-haired cats are mated directly to Siamese the dominant genes produce short-haired, solid-coloured cats. However the recessive characteristics of long hair and point markings are still carried and in the next generation about 1 in 16 of the kittens has long fur and Siamese markings. They then have to be further bred to produce a good Persian type with a cobby look and full coat.

In Britain this was done by breeding with further longhairs of good quality and, since Black and Blue Longhairs were prominent in the breeding programme the first colours to be recognized were Seal and Blue. In America the new type closest to the required look were bred together. In Britain all the colours are grouped in one class but in the United States there are separate show classes for each colour of Himalayan.

The Colourpoint Longhairs and the Himalayans have low cobby bodies set on short, sturdy legs. The round head is set on a short, thick neck and has a short nose, full cheeks, round eyes and low-set ears. The eyes are always brilliant blue, whatever the colour of the cat. The fur is long, thick and soft with a full frill over the neck and chest, a luxuriant tail and tufts in the ears and between the toes. The face, legs, ears and tail are of darker fur, set off against a pale body colour as in the Siamese.

Seal Colourpoint Longhair (Seal Point Himalayan)
The coat of this variety should be pale fawn to cream

Seal Point Himalayan/Colourpoint Longhair

215

shading gradually into a lighter colour on the stomach and chest, with points of dark seal brown. Nose leather and paw pads match the points.

Chocolate Point Himalayan/Colourpoint Longhair

Blue Point Himalayan/Colourpoint Longhair

Blue Colourpoint Longhair (Blue Point Himalayan)
The body colour is a glacial bluish white which shades to white on the stomach and chest and the points are blue. Nose leather and paw pads are slate blue.

Chocolate Colourpoint Longhair (Chocolate Point Himalayan) has an ivory body colour with no shading and points of warm toned milk chocolate. Nose leather and paw pads are pink in America and match the points in Britain.

216

Red Colourpoint Longhair (Red Point or Flame Point Himalayan) The Red has an off-white body colour. The Cat Fanciers Association call this colour flame and ask for points of delicate orange flame on a creamy white body. Nose leather and paw pads are pink.

Lilac Colourpoint Longhair (Lilac Himalayan) This variety of the Colourpoint/Himalayan has a cold glacial-coloured body, magnolia according to

Lilac Point Himalayan/ Colourpoint Longhair

Red Point Himalayan/Colourpoint Longhair

217

the British standard, with frost grey points that have a pinkish tone. Nose leather and paw pads are lilac or lavender pink, or pink in the case of the paw pads in America. The eyes are blue.

Cream Colourpoint Longhair With a body of white shading to palest cream, rich cream points, pink nose leather and paw pads and blue eyes, this is a recognized variety in Britain but not in America.

Blue Cream Colourpoint Longhair (Blue Cream Himalayan) In this cat the points are blue with patches of cream and the body colour is bluish or creamy white, shading to white on the underparts. Nose leather and paw pads are slate blue and/or pink and the eyes a vivid blue.

218

Lilac Cream Colourpoint Longhair (Lilac Cream Himalayan) The lilac and cream patching, like the Chocolate Cream, is not accepted by all associations. Nose leather and paw pads are lavender and/or pink and the eyes blue.

Chocolate Tortie Colourpoint Longhair (Chocolate Cream Himalayan) Here chocolate pairs with cream in the colour patching of the points in a variety that is

**Lilac Cream
Himalayan/Colourpoint Longhair**

**Blue Cream Himalayan
Colourpoint Longhair**

**Chocolate Tortie
Himalayan/Colourpoint Longhair**

Seal Lynx Point Himalayan

Tortoiseshell Himalayan/Colourpoint Longhair

recognized in Britain and by some American associations. Leather and paw pads are brown and/or cream and the eyes a vivid blue.

Tortoiseshell Colourpoint Longhair (Tortie Point Himalayan) The British standard limits the points in the Tortie to seal with a cream (instead of white) body colour. The Cat Fanciers Association specifies seal, red and cream, but some standards allow for only red and cream and in the points. Nose leather and paw pads are pink and/or seal and the eyes blue.

Lynx Point Himalayan Some American associations accept a tabby-pointed Himalayan, with appropriate coloured nose leather and paw pads, in seal, chocolate, lilac, blue and red. All have blue eyes.

Other Himalayans Some American associations place solid-coloured chocolate and lilac longhairs among the Himalayans. These are described on page 187.

Red Lynx Point Himalayan

Blue Lynx Point Himalayan

BIRMAN

The Birman, also known as the Sacred Cat of Burma, has a romantic legend to explain its appearance. Centuries ago, even before the time of the Buddha, 100 pure white cats were kept in the Khmer temple of Lao-Tsun in Burma, where the blue-eyed golden goddess Tsun-Kyan-Kse was worshipped. One night Thai invaders attacked the temple and the priests asked the goddess for her help. As they gathered before her, invoking her protection, the elderly chief priest Mun-Ha died. As his spirit left him, his particular cat leaped upon his head and everyone saw the cat's white fur change to the gold of the goddess and its eyes become her sapphire blue, while the ears and paws took on the colour of fertile earth, except where they touched the old priest's silver hair. The spirit of Mun-Ha then passed into the cat (see page 112), which turned from the goddess to face the approaching invaders, inspiring the other priests to fight and save their temple. (Another version has Mun-Ha struck down by an invader before the miracle rallies the priests to fight.) Next morning all the temple cats had taken on the goddess's sacred colouring.

In 1919 two descendants of these cats were presented to French soldiers who had helped to protect a temple of Lao-Tsun during a rebellion. One cat died on its way to France, but the other, a female, was already pregnant and her kittens established the breed in Europe.

Some insist on a more prosaic explanation of the Birman's origins and say it was created by French breeders from Siamese and long-haired black and whites. What is unquestionable is that the breed was recognized in France in 1925. It was not until the 1960s that they were introduced into Britain, recognition coming in 1966, and in America in 1967.

The Birman's conformation is not like other long-haired cats. Its body is long, though stocky, and set on heavy medium-length legs, with short strong paws. Its tail is longer and slimmer than the Persian, its head round with full cheeks – the Cat Fanciers Association standard says the forehead slopes back and is slightly convex and asks for a Roman nose and a slight flat spot just in front of the ears. This is certainly not the wedge-shaped Siamese face, so

Seal Point Birman

Blue Point Birman

though superficially the Birman may look like the Himalayan or the Balinese it has distinctly different proportions from either type. More immediately noticeable is the difference in the markings. The Siamese-type pattern is here varied by the addition of white feet. The American standard specifies that the white shall extend up to an even line across the paw at the third joint of the front paws and on the back it covers the entire paw, extending up the back of the leg to end in a point like a gauntlet. The silky fur is not so full as in the Persian, though with a good ruff and bushy tail. It curls slightly on the belly.

Sealpoint Birman The original colour form, showing the goddess's colours as seal points but with a warm cream to pale fawn coat – the British standard describes it as beige that is slightly golden – with seal nose leather and pink paw pads.

Chocolate Point Birman

Lilac Point Birman

Blue Point Birman In America a bluish white body colour is preferred for this variety, in Britain the same warm colour as the Seal. The points are blue grey and the nose leather slate, with pink pads in America.

Chocolate Point Birman, recognized in America, but not yet in Britain, has an ivory body colour with no shading and chocolate points. Nose leather is cinnamon pink and paw pads are pink.

Lilac Point Birman has a cold, glacial, near white coat and frost grey points with a pinkish tone. Nose leather is lavender pink and paw pads are pink. It is not yet recognized in Britain.

RAGDOLL

As first recognized in 1965, this American breed looked like a Birman in physique and coat but both dark pawed and bi-coloured forms have now been accepted. However, it is not their appearance that gives Ragdolls their individuality, though they tend to be large cats with thick fur. The first examples were kittens born to a Persian female after she was badly injured in an accident. They all had a unique disposition: placid and limp like a rag doll. It is claimed that they feel no pain and do not fight. It has been suggested that this was in some way the result of the accident to their mother, but that is contrary to all accepted genetic principles. It was originally said that they had no sense of danger but they have been shown to hide or crouch when frightened.

Blue Point Ragdoll (gloved)

Ragdolls are said to accept leash training and they like being handled, but must be treated carefully since their insensitivity to pain makes them vulnerable to injury. Their original breeder, who set up an association to control their sale and breeding, described them as 'the closest one can get to a real live baby and have an animal.' Such dependency may seem to others totally contrary to what they admire in a cat and there is considerable controversy about the breed, which is not recognized in Britain.

The pointed coat may be seal, blue, chocolate or lilac and a slight white nose streak and white tip to the tail may be present in the original form of the cat. Kittens do not develop their full colour until about two years old. It has been claimed that their fur is non-matting and requires little or no grooming.

Seal Point Ragdoll   **Red Bi-colour Ragdoll**

SOMALI

A long-haired version of the Abyssinian, this breed was developed from the occasional longhair that occurred in Abyssinian litters, result of a recessive gene for long hair that was carried in certain lines. It has exactly the same lithe physique as the Abyssinian, with a long body, a slightly rounded, wedge-shaped head with large, pointed ears and almond-shaped eyes and a long tail, which is thick at the base and tapering. The coat is agouti-ticked with Abyssinian face-markings, darker legs and tail tip, but it is long and silky-textured, with prominent ear tufts, a generous ruff and 'breeches' and a plume-like tail.

Because the fur is very much longer than that of the Abyssinian it carries many more bands of ticking - probably ten or more on each hair, and the colour tends to appear much deeper and richer than in the short-haired cat. Kittens are usually born very dark in colour and it takes about 18 months for the full ticked colouring to develop. The fur is not woolly and is therefore easy to groom.

Somalis tend to have gentle temperaments and soft voices. They have had championship status in America since 1978 but have been given only preliminary standards in Britain.

Ruddy (Usual) Somali gives the impression of an orange brown coat. The underside, chest and inside of the legs are an even ruddy tone, with dark tipping extending down from the head and spine. There should be no rings on the tail but the dark spine line runs down it to end in a black tip. Nose leather is tile red and paw pads are black or brown. Eyes are gold or green.

Red (Sorrel) Somali has a warm red coat, tipped with chocolate brown. Nose leather is rosy pink and paw pads are pink with chocolate brown between the toes. Eyes are gold or green.

Red (Sorrel) Somali

Ruddy (Usual) Somali

TIFFANY

The Tiffany is a long-haired version of the Burmese, combining the Burmese conformation with a long, silky coat and maintaining the brown coloration of the Burmese, although the colouring is usually a little lighter than in the short-haired cat. Kittens are born a light coffee colour and the long fur and the richer light sable coat develop together as they mature. Nose leather and paw pads are rich brown. Eyes are golden in the adult cat.

Tiffany

BALINESE

The graceful Balinese does not come from Bali, but its dainty feet and waving plume of a tail reminded one of the original breeders of that island's dancers and thus it gained its name. A Siamese cat with long fur that occurred spontaneously in Siamese litters, it is not the result of cross-breeding, though this is sometimes disputed by those who think it an unlikely mutation and that at some time longhair must have been introduced into the bloodline.

Whatever the reason, the result is an extremely beautiful and elegant cat. It was first recognized in America in 1970 and has an enthusiastic following in Britain where a provisional standard has now been established. It is a dainty cat, with long svelte lines and a long wedge-shaped head. The Cat Fanciers Association standard specifies that the wedge starts at the nose and flares out to the tips of the ears to form a triangle, with no break at the whiskers and not less than the width of an eye between the eyes. The large, pointed ears continue the angle of the wedge and the almond shaped eyes slope at an harmonious angle.

The coat is long, fine and silky (though not so long as in the Persian) and has no downy undercoat. The British standard describes it as lying flat along the body except around the chin, neck and tail, but prefers it to lack a frill so that the underlying bone structure is not excessively obscured. The colour points are as in the Siamese. In America Seal Point, Chocolate Point, Blue Point and Lilac Point are the

Seal Point Balinese

colours recognized, others being known as Javanese, but in Britain the whole range of British Siamese colour varieties are possible within the breed.

Seal Point Balinese has a body colour of pale fawn to warm cream, shading to lighter on the stomach and chest, with deep seal brown points, nose leather and paw pads. Eyes are deep vivid blue.

Chocolate Point Balinese has a body colour of unshaded ivory with warm milk chocolate points and cinammon-pink nose leather and paw pads. Eyes are deep blue.

Blue Point Balinese has a body colour of bluish white, cold in tone and shading to white on the chest and stomach. Points are deep blue and paw pads and nose leather slate. Eyes are vivid blue.

Lilac Point Balinese In America glacial white body colour with no shading is matched to frosty grey points with a pinkish tone. In Britain the body colour is magnolia and some shading is accepted. Nose leather and paw pads are lavender pink and eyes a vivid blue.

Red Point Balinese have a white body with perhaps slight apricot shading and points of

Chocolate Point Balinese

Blue Point Balinese

Lilac Point Balinese

Red Point Balinese

reddish gold which, like most red cats, often still show faint tabby marks. Nose and paws are red, eyes blue.

Cream Point Balinese have a white body colour with points of pale cream, pink nose leather and paw pads and blue eyes.

Tortie Point Balinese have body colour, nose leather and paw pads to match that of the main colour in their tortie pattern and blue eyes.

Tabby Point Balinese come in all the range of tabby colours described for the Siamese with appropriate paws pads and nose leather.

JAVANESE

This breed, named after the mainland west of Bali, is the classification given in America to those long-haired cats of Siamese type with colours and markings which are not accepted as Balinese (just as they are not accepted in the Siamese but known as Colorpoints and Oriental Shorthairs). In Britain these cats are grouped with the Balinese.

**Blue Tabby Point Balinese/
Blue Lynx Point Javanese**

Tortie Point Balinese/Javanese

235

CYMRIC (MANX LONGHAIR)

It was not until the 1960s that breeders finding long-haired cats which appeared in some North American Manx litters decided to develop them as a separate breed and gained recognition for it under the name Cymric (the Welsh word for Welsh) from the Canadian Cat Association, and later as the Manx Longhair in the United States. The double coat is medium length and softer than that of the normal Manx, but it has the same conformation with long back legs, no tail and the final vertebrae missing and all the other Manx characteristics. In America it is known in the same colour varieties as the Manx, but it is not yet recognized in Britain.

Silver Tabby Cymric

Index of Breeds and Varieties

237

238